To Alan.
Best Wishes

Gareth
Chilcott

95

Gareth Chilcott

Gareth Chilcott

My Favourite Rugby Stories

GARETH CHILCOTT
with
LES SCOTT

Illustrations by David Farris

SIMON & SCHUSTER
LONDON · SYDNEY · NEW YORK · TOKYO · SINGAPORE · TORONTO

First published in Great Britain by Simon & Schuster Ltd, 1995
A Viacom Company

Simon & Schuster Ltd
West Garden Place
Kendal Street
London W2 2AQ

Simon & Schuster of Australia Pty Ltd
Sydney

A CIP catalogue record for this book is available
from the British Library

ISBN 0-671-71425-2

Typeset in Perpetua 13/15pt by
Palimpsest Book Production Limited, Polmont, Stirlingshire
Printed and bound in Great Britain by
Butler & Tanner, Frome and London

Acknowledgements

Grateful thanks to the following, without whom . . .

Ann and Chloe, for literally everything and helping me through the difficult times. Now that we are a family and I am so busy, I rarely get through *The Sunday Times*.

Caroline and the families in Sunderland and Eccleshall. 'He's written a number of books. Some better than others. We think he's working on one of the others at the moment.'

Nick Simcock, who did the lion's share of the research for this book. He is so thorough that he came up with not only the the teams and scorers for the 1986 France — England game in Paris but the names and addresses of the crowd as well.

Martin Fletcher, for his renowned expertise and for giving us the 'green light'. A very good scrum half on his day. Unfortunately for Martin's own rugby career, his day was a Sunday.

Jacquie Clare, for her invaluable expertise and guidance, and Caroline North for similar.

Richard Hill, England's most capped scrum-half, whose memory helped fill in the gaps. Now an independent financial adviser and the reason I'm always on the road. Every time he hears I've spoken at a dinner, he sells me another policy.

Mazda UK, for making sure I travel in style, safety and absolute comfort when on the road.

The *Daily Star*, for their help and regular coverage of rugby — even when the Five Nations is not being played.

Paul Moors and Marianne Day, for their wonderful support. They also support Stoke City AFC — talk about martyrs to causes.

Jack Rowell, for shaping me. What a job he made of it!

David Farris, for the cartoons. A man with plenty of lead in his pencil.

Jo and Jordan Bailey. For all their warmth and friendship. Cool? They fill their bird bath with Perrier water.

And all those who helped when times were tough. You know who you are!

Contents

Five Nations Tales

Tours

Fitness, Tactics and Training

The Great Characters

The Game Now, Then and in the Future

Contents

To Les Scott.

George Best is right when he says Les must be the most compulsive tea drinker in the country. He is also, to my mind, one of our most entertaining and versatile writers. I'd like to convey my thanks to him for collaborating with me on this book. His advice and considerable humour made the writing a pleasure. Thanks, Les. Brew?

Gareth Chilcott

Bristol, 1995

Introduction

H ISTORY HAS it that the game of rugby was invented in 1823 at Rugby School. Whilst playing a game of football during a games lesson, a forward called William Webb Ellis picked up the ball and ran with it in his hands, bobbing and weaving to avoid tackles from the opposition. Rubbish!

I'm well aware that by refuting this story I am, not for the first time, mind you, ruffling the feathers of one or two people at HQ and getting up the noses of those who hold rugby's traditions close to their hearts. The William Webb Ellis theory is so widely held as being true by the rugby powers that be that in 1987 they went and named the inaugural Rugby World Cup trophy after him – a well-intended, but misplaced, conception. Let us look at the evidence.

Any boy taking part in a PE lesson who spoils for other children whatever game is being played with a gross act of stupidity stemming from the fact that he is the only one who doesn't know the rules would be lambasted by the teacher and ridiculed to hell by his classmates. Webb Ellis was probably one of those PE phobics who always had a note from his mother asking for him to be excused games; who, on the odd occasion when he did deign to participate, huddled in a corner of the changing room when removing his trousers, fearful that another lad should catch sight of his willy and want to know why he had one whilst other boys did not.

Only such a boy would be stupid enough to ruin a perfectly good, fluid attacking soccer move by picking up the ball and running with it. I'm convinced that Webb Ellis did it only because he hadn't been attending PE lessons and therefore didn't know the rules of soccer. He probably went to this particular lesson only to appease his long-suffering parents. Lo and behold, the last boy to be chosen for any side receives the credit for inventing the world's greatest team game. I ask you, what tosh!

Imagine the scene. Webb Ellis picks up the ball and starts to run with it. The other boys moan at his stupidity, but the PE master hesitates as he goes to blow his whistle.

'You peanut brain!' Webb Ellis's classmates howl in derision.

'Hang on, boys,' the master shouts to his jeering fourth-formers. 'Stop your heckling. I think young Webb Ellis might have something here.'

As if.

The other flaw in the theory that William Webb Ellis was the first man to play rugby is the description of him being a forward who 'picked up the ball and ran with it in his hands, bobbing and weaving to avoid tackles from the opposition'.

As a forward myself who played top-class rugby for seventeen years for the British Lions, England and probably the most successful club side in the world, let me tell you, I have seen one or two things on a rugby pitch – but a forward who runs with the ball in his hands and bobs and weaves avoiding tackles from the opposition? This I have never seen.

Not content to base my conclusions on my own experiences, I asked around. Wade Dooley, Brian Moore, Bob Norster, Dean Richards, Nick Popplewell. Not one of them can ever recall seeing a forward, in any standard of rugby, doing such a reckless and outlandish thing.

From reading this far, you might have gained the impression that I have scant regard for one or two of the sacred cows in rugby. Absolutely right. So if this book is not intended to expound the traditions of rugby, then what is it about? Following the Pilkington Cup final at Twickenham in 1992 the Bath players enjoyed to the full the post-match celebrations. As they say in Ireland, the crack was good. We players swapped favourite rugby tales and anecdotes, some of which were based on personal experience. Some we had been told by opponents, both at club and international level. The stories all had two things in common: they were true and they were funny.

As we travelled back to Bath, I passed part of the journey by listing as many humorous rugby tales as I could remember from my career. It occurred to me that if players enjoyed listening to them, many rugby fans may like to hear them too. I had it in my mind to put them some day into a book that would capture the true spirit of the game: the fun, warmth and the 'crack'.

As luck would have it, in 1994 I met writer Les Scott at a sporting dinner. Les had just finished working with soccer legend George Best on a book of George's favourite soccer stories for publishers Simon & Schuster. Would I be interested in writing a book of my favourite rugby tales? 'Does Judith Chalmers have a passport?' I replied.

In the months that followed we met often to collaborate and write, sometimes at his offices, sometimes at mine; in executive boxes in the Teacher's Stand at Bath; following sporting dinners; in hotel cocktail bars; in TV studios – and even on the terraces at Orrell.

How far I have managed to capture the spirit of rugby and the 'crack' is for you, the reader, to decide. I'd like to think this book is one of those you can pick up and dip into again and again, reacquainting yourself with your own favourite stories much as you would with old friends.

One word of advice. When you do pick up this book again, whatever you do, don't start running with it. You could be credited with inventing a new sport — and that would never do.

I hope you enjoy it.

Gareth Chilcott
Bristol
September 1995

Early Days

'My impressions of our first training session?
It would have been encouraging if some of
you could have broken out into a jog.'

*Jack Rowell, former Bath and current England manager –
coach.*

'The best time to be successful is now.'

Ian McGeechan, former Scotland coach.

1

Small World

ARRIVING AT Bath Rugby Union Football Club for the very
first time in 1976 produced one of those coincidental
meetings that, although no one realised it at the time, would
have far-reaching consequences for all and sundry. Perhaps not
as globally profound as when Mr Rolls met Mr Royce, but it
certainly changed my life.

Before I tell you of how I met the man who would transform
me irrevocably and in whose rugby plans and ambitions I would
be a cornerstone, let me first of all tell you about how I came
to be invited to join Bath.

I attended Aston Park Comprehensive School in Bristol and
was no angel. I was always in trouble. In my fourth year I
was caned by a teacher called Mr Ridgeway for persistent
impertinence and disruption in the metalwork class. Even in
those days I had a great instinct for personal survival and as he
left the room to fetch the cane from the deputy headmaster's
office I pushed a sheet of tin down the seat of my pants. When
he returned he gave me four swift strokes across my rear end
and half the class got up and walked out because they thought
the bell had gone.

The only two subjects in which I took any real interest
were PE and English. No matter what the sport, I'd have a

go at it. I relished the challenge of applying my (even in those days) not inconsiderable physical strength to the task in hand. Soccer, basketball, cricket, cross-country running, track and field athletics, volleyball, badminton, swimming – I had a go at them all. In fact the only thing I didn't play much of was rugby. My school had little time for rugby on the PE curriculum as it was a comprehensive ensconced in the heart of a working-class soccer-mad area. English, the other subject I liked, appealed to me because I enjoyed reading stories, books and plays – it attracted the storyteller and actor in me. Don't get me wrong, though, I was no Melvyn Bragg. My knowledge of literature and plays wasn't deep, but at least I knew that Sherlock Holmes wasn't sheltered housing for senior citizens.

Saturday afternoons were spent on the terraces of Ashton Gate supporting Bristol City. In those days City were managed by Alan Dicks, who went on to take them up into the First Division, or Premiership as it is now, in 1976. City never had the wherewithal or financial clout to stay there and were eventually relegated. It was at this time that I received my first lesson in how fickle fans can be. Gaining promotion had been a wonderful achievement by Alan Dicks, especially considering the size of the club, yet a few years later, when things did not work out, the supporters turned against him. What compounded the embarrassment for me was when they'd call for his removal by chanting from the terraces 'Dicks out!'

When I left school at the age of fifteen in 1973 I had little in the way of qualifications and even less in the way of ambition. I immediately signed on the dole. I had been unemployed for some eight months and was associating with what could be termed a dodgy crowd, a bunch of lads who had been on the dole for far longer than I. So long, in fact, that they had ceased being simply unemployed and had become unemployable. These youths had also fallen into the trap of taking drugs to relieve their tedium and boredom. It was one

Friday morning, when I was hanging around a street corner as usual and saw one of the crowd, high on heaven knows what, chasing a Polo wrapper which was blowing down the street and shouting, 'Stop it, someone, it's my Giro!' that I knew I had to escape.

As luck would have it, in 1974 I came across my old teacher, Mr Ridgeway, again whilst walking through Bristol city centre. I had given Norman Ridgeway a fairly hard time at school as I had been such a demotivated pupil. As we chatted I was moved by the genuine interest and care he showed for my wellbeing. Far from bearing any animosity towards me, Norman expressed concern at the fact that I seemed to be drifting aimlessly. He told me I needed some purpose in life, that I needed to belong. I listened intently to what he had to say. He was right. I did feel I needed to be a part of something. But what?

Norman went on to tell me he was involved with Old Redcliffians, a strong Bristol combination rugby club, and suggested that it might hold some interest for me. Partly because I had nothing better to do and partly because my respect for Norman was growing, I agreed to attend a training session with the 'Old Reds', as they are known. It was one of the best decisions of my life.

After a few training sessions I made it into the Old Redcliffians Under-18 XV as a hooker. A short while later they moved me to tight-head prop, a position many players prefer because it allows you to have both shoulders in contact with the opposition, while at loose head you have only one.

Life with the 'Old Reds' was just what I needed. The club consisted mainly of people who worked down at Bristol docks, so there was none of the aloofness or snobbery one can find at one or two clubs even today. It was here that I discovered rugby was full of colourful characters. Pete the Diesel Fitter had played for the Old Reds for some years. One night at training I found out that he was a crane operator in the main warehouse at the dockside.

'A crane operator? Then why do they call you Pete the Diesel Fitter?' I asked.

'Because when everyone has gone home,' Pete said impishly, 'I wander through the warehouse and rummage through any crates of clothing that are damaged and open saying, "Diesel fit the wife".' or "Diesel fit the daughter-in-law".'

We trained every Tuesday and Thursday night and I quickly realised that at last I had found an outlet for all my pent-up physical energy. After a game Saturday evening would be spent downing a few pints. I made friends, I felt I was wanted and I felt I belonged. Having to attend training regularly, on time, and totally apply myself to the physical tasks we were set brought discipline into my life. Away fixtures took me out of Bristol. For the first time in my life I was seeing different towns and meeting people from places such as Lichfield, Peterborough and Wolverhampton – hardly glamorous, I know, but when you were a seventeen-year-old who had spent countless hours hanging around the dole office and street corners, believe you me, Saturdays were really something to look forward to. My mother used to say, 'The devil will find work for idle hands.' I reckon I escaped from the street corners just in time.

I was meeting people from all walks of life and I loved it. For one who had played little rugby at school, my game came on in leaps and bounds. During the summer of 1975 I was invited to attend training at Bristol. This was a great step forward for me because Bristol were then, as they are today, one of the top club sides in England. In 1973 they had played Coventry in the National Knock-Out Cup final and in men like John Pullin, Alan Morley and Dave Rollitt they boasted players who had represented England in the Five Nations.

Not many people know I played for Bristol, simply because I have never made much of it. Without putting too fine a point on it, I did not enjoy my short spell there. Old Redcliffians adhered to the adage 'All for one and one for all.' At Bristol, however, there appeared to be numerous cliques. The first-team players and the second XV – the United side, as they are called – got on with one another about as well as Alan Sugar and Terry Venables. They were forever glaring at one another and the unspoken message seemed to be: 'Bastards, you're not getting our first-team places.' The Bristol first XV looked upon players from the other sides in the club with contempt. As the new boy I was about as welcome as a fart in spacesuit. Only a handful of the fourth-team players deigned to speak to me. After a week or so the secretary did manage to ask to me if I wanted to go back to Old Redcliffians. My reply was succinct. 'Does a bear shit in the woods?'

As the preparations for the 1975–6 season got underway at the Old Reds, I was invited to attend Bath for a trial period. The Bristol experience had disillusioned me about life at a top-class rugby club, but my team-mates at the Old Reds told me that Bath was much more sociable and friendly. At that time Bath were not the force in rugby that they are today and lived in the shadow of the more successful south-west clubs. Any player who could not get into the Bristol or Gloucester first XVs would turn his attention to Bath, and the club were happy to accept such players. For me, however, it was another big step up in the world of rugby. Far from being resentful of the attention I was being given, my Old Reds team-mates actively encouraged me to give it one more go at a big club. If I hadn't known them better, I would have thought they were trying to get rid of me!

At this stage I was still on the dole and didn't have a car, so for my first training session with Bath I caught a bus from Bristol into Bath town centre and looked for another bus out to the training ground. It was raining and as I went to cross the road at the traffic lights a large Mercedes swished by through a puddle and literally soaked me. I was fuming. Seeing the lights change to red, I sprinted up to the car to give the driver a piece of my mind.

I banged on his window and, taking the right leg of my trousers in my hand, showed him the extent of my drenching. The driver, a silver-haired business-type gent in his early forties, was most apologetic. He offered to run me where I wanted to go, but I was not to be placated. I told him in no uncertain terms what he could do with his big car.

'Impossible. Even my arse isn't that big,' he said in a broad north-east accent.

The lights changed again and I left him with the impression that I gravely doubted his parentage as he pulled off and I ran to catch my bus.

When I arrived at the Lambridge Ground, where Bath train, I found Clive Howard, the club secretary. Clive informed me that Bath's newly appointed coach was starting his duties that night and that, as a 'fellow new boy', he would take me to meet him.

My knees turned to jelly as Clive took me into the coach's office. There, seated behind the desk, was the man with whom I had had the altercation at the traffic lights.

'We've met,' said Jack Rowell as John introduced me. 'Young Mr Chilcott has a keen vocabulary and, dare I say it, a dry humour.'

'Small world,' I said nervously.

'Yes, it is,' said Jack, sitting back in his chair. 'But I wouldn't like to paint it.'

'What should I call you?' I asked, wondering whether he preferred to be called Coach, as most club coaches do, or Jack, if, like some, he favoured the more informal approach.

'After you've been through one of my training sessions, sonny,' he snarled, standing up to his full height of 6ft 4ins, 'you'll be calling me Evil Bastard. Now welcome to Bath!'

2

Poor Relations

T HE AREA around Gloucester, Bath and Bristol is the hub of a
hotbed of English rugby. As the north-east and Merseyside
produce football nuts, so the south-west spawns rugby fanatics.
Nowadays, in the league set-up – and this is not including
Courage League clubs – the South and South-West Division of
the pyramid system has twenty-two divisions. That's 286 clubs,
and there are literally hundreds of smaller ones which have yet
to get on to the league ladder. What is more, each of these clubs
runs between three and nine sides every weekend. Whichever
way you look at it, that's one hell of a lot of rugby.

Little wonder, then, that in the first eight years of the
Courage Leagues the First Division title was won five times
by a side from the south-west, and that since the inception of
the original John Player Cup in 1971–2 (now the Pilkington
Cup), clubs from the south-west area have won this prestigious
trophy no fewer than fourteen times up to 1995. The fact that
my club, Bath, have appeared in most finals (nine), winning
all of them, gives me immense pride and satisfaction. Add
the fact that Bath is the side which has won those five
Courage League titles and you can see why the rep who
sells silver polish drops a bottle of whisky off at the club
every Christmas.

I consider myself very fortunate to have played in seven of those Pilkington Cup finals, a feat bettered only by my best pal, Richard Hill, who has appeared in eight, the last in 1994, when Bath beat Leicester 21–9. It was Richard's last game in Bath colours, for in the weeks before he had announced his retirement. The final drew a world-record crowd for a club match of 60,000, and Richard maintains that they all turned up just to say goodbye to him.

Considering my disciplinary record, I am proud to say I was never sent off in a Cup final. Nigel Horton (Moseley, in 1972), Bob Mordell (Rosslyn Park, 1976) and John Gadd (Gloucester, 1990), unfortunately for them, jointly hold that dubious record. I never had as much as a ticking-off by a referee, either, which is saying something when you remember the pressure and what is at stake.

From 1984 to the present, then, has been a golden and glorious period for Bath, but it wasn't always so. When Jack Rowell and I arrived at the Recreation Ground in 1976, Bath were very much the poor relations of south-west rugby, never mind English rugby.

Business was the reason Jack Rowell left his native north-east for Avon. Under his guidance Newcastle Gosforth had become a force in English rugby. He was, and remains, an ambitious man and on arriving in the Avon area he immediately set about looking for a job as coach at a club which was equally ambitious. Clifton were on the look-out for a coach at the time. They didn't so much interview Jack – rather, he interviewed them. In the end he decided that, although Clifton were a lovely club with great people, they were not ambitious enough for him.

Bath were formed as far back as 1865, so they were hardly experiencing growing pains. In the mid-seventies, however, they were drifting aimlessly, as I say, very much poor relations to the Bristols and Gloucesters of this world. They did, though, have three things going for them: they were very ambitious;

they were a club that had great potential; and thirdly, and perhaps most importantly, the committee were prepared to let Jack get on with his job as manager-coach whilst they busied themselves with theirs. These were the factors that persuaded Jack that Bath was the club for him. Jack's drive, ambition and, even then, renowned coaching ability, left Bath, for their part, in no doubt that he was their man. It was a marriage made in heaven.

Some coaches get lucky. They inherit or have selected for them a team that consists of good players. You don't really have to tell a good rugby player what to do out on the park; he knows. You send them all out and, as long as you have a balanced side, they will perform well.

Roger Uttley, Jack's predecessor with England during my international career, was in truth an overrated coach. He was lucky enough to have players such as Rob Andrew, Wade Dooley, Dean Richards, Mike Teague, Mickey Skinner, Richard Hill, Jon Webb and Peter Winterbottom in his side. A Bristol grandmother could have sent out players of that calibre on to a pitch and they'd have got a result to make her look a competent coach. We were a good England side but, with a top-class international coach, we would have been a great side.

We players used to call Roger 'the Timekeeper' because he was obsessed with time. 'What shall we do? Twenty minutes of scrummaging?' he would ask us. Scrummaging over, he would look at his watch. 'What shall we do now? Fifteen minutes of running the ball?'

That done, he took another glance at his watch. 'What shall we do now? Ten minutes on line-outs?'

We players had a laugh about it in the England hotel as we sat down to the Friday-evening meal before a game against Ireland. 'What shall we do now, Coach? Twenty minutes of eating?' asked Mickey Skinner, checking his watch.

As the England coach Roger should have been telling us what to do, not asking us. He was a good motivator but he never sussed the weaknesses of the opposition, never told individual players what they had to do in certain positions or situations. What is more, he never stood by his players. If the press or, more importantly, the RFU selectors had a downer on one of them he never backed him.

Hugo MacNeill, the great Dublin and Oxford Universities, Blackrock and London Irish full-back who won thirty-seven caps for his country, is a man whose opinion I hold in high regard. Following England's 25–20 victory over Ireland at Twickenham in 1986, I was chatting with him about the differences between the selection of the respective teams.

'The difference between England and Ireland is that I've had a poor game today but I'll play for Ireland in the next international. If I was English I wouldn't be in the next England team. The Irish coach and selectors stick with their players when they go through a bad patch. Have one bad game for England and you're out.'

Hugo had a point. I think that season England used forty-eight players! The great sides of that time, such as Australia, used around eighteen to twenty players a season and the changes they made were in the main due to injuries. Fortunately, England are not as fickle in their selections these days – in fact, in the 1995 Five Nations, they started all four matches with an unchanged team.

Jack Rowell is different. He knows and understands that leadership is action, not just position. He took over a mediocre club side which contained one or two good players and eventually transformed Bath into the most successful club side the world has ever known.

After seeing Bath in action in a couple of games Jack offered his verdict one night at training. 'You're like a lighthouse in the desert. Occasional flashes of brilliance but, in the main, bloody useless.'

He examined the club's playing strength from top to bottom. Unlike a lot of clubs, Bath run four sides: the first XV; the second XV, which goes under the name of Bath United; the third XV, known as Bath Spartans; and an under-21 side.

Irish John was a player who had been going through the motions with the Spartans for a couple of seasons without ever making his mark. If there was anybody better available, that person played. If not, Irish John was called in and went through the motions for eighty minutes. He'd stand about for most of the match, and though he made an occasional run he needed ten minutes to recover. He did all his training in the bar with his right arm. Jack Rowell had watched the Spartans for all of ten minutes when he made his first judgment.

'Irish John's going to have to go for a start. There's no place at this club any more for his sort of player,' he said.

'But how could the Spartans ever replace John?' a selector asked.

'Just go down to the mortuary and open any drawer,' replied Jack.

Jack and the first XV captain Jim Waterman broke with tradition straight away. At the time Bath, like every other rugby club, trained on Tuesday and Thursday nights. This was changed to Monday and Wednesday and remains the case to this day. The theory was that players would do all their hard work in training in pre-season and top this up with a hard session every six weeks or so. The twice-weekly sessions would then focus on tactics on Monday, followed by a medium work-out on a Wednesday, allowing the players to rest up fresh for Saturday. Training on a Wednesday instead of a Thursday also provided an extra twenty-four hours for anyone with minor knocks and pulls to recover.

Before Jack's arrival the Bath training had been far from

methodical. It consisted of more or less the same routines every night: a warm-up, some stretching exercises and shuttle runs followed by a game, then a few laps around the pitch. If players wanted to work out in the weights room then it was up to them. Jack and his assistants Tom Hudson and Dave Robson changed all that. First of all, to improve our fitness levels, training was upped to three nights a week. There was no quibble with those who didn't like it – they were welcome to leave. You either did it or you found another club. The thing is, when you've done a day's work, put in a hard training session three nights a week on icy mud with sleet coming at you virtually horizontally, then given your all on a Saturday, you're not fit for much else. It came as a shock to the regular Bath players.

One night Jim Waterman's son was doing his biology homework and asked his seemingly eternally weary dad if he knew what a condom was. 'Of course I know,' said Jim. 'I've been carrying one around in my wallet for months.'

Jack, Tom and Dave also wanted to change Bath's reputation as a haven for Bristol or Gloucester cast-offs, a third-choice club. They wanted top players to want to come to Bath, to make it the club everyone aspired to. They nurtured the idea that there would come a day when to play for Bath meant you had reached the top in English club rugby. It took some time but in the end the club reached that pinnacle and stayed there.

Jack, Tom, Dave and successive captains Jim Waterman, Mike Beese and Roger Spurrell gave Bath and their players pride. They also turned what had been a fragmented club into a family. One of the ways they did this was by reorganising the bars.

At the time Bath had more bars than Bristol prison. There was a Committee Bar, Players' Bar, United and Spartans' Bar, Supporters' bar, Club Members' Bar, Veterans' Bar, Public Bar, Press Bar – and those are only the ones I can remember! They were all ripped out in favour of just two: the Members' and

Non-Members' bars. Even then the demarcation between them did not matter a great deal, and it still doesn't today. So the supporter who paid his money to watch his side on a Saturday and fancied a pint or two afterwards would find him or herself standing at the bar next to internationals such as John Horton, Simon Halliday, Richard Hill or myself. And why not?

The upshot was that the club started to develop a real family atmosphere. The people of Bath who had been sitting by their firesides for years waiting for a reason to come down to the Recreation Ground started to turn up in great numbers. Men, women and children were made to feel not only welcome but part of the set-up. In the mid-seventies Bath's average attendance was a few hundred. Gradually, season by season, it rose and now, in the mid-nineties, it is around 6,000 and we have over 9,000 club memberships – people from every walk of life, colour, race and creed.

In those embryonic days leather rugby balls were still in common use as opposed to the moulded plastic Gilbert balls we see today. Bath hadn't the money for lavish equipment. The leather rugby balls we used in training were so old, lacerated and tattered that every time you jumped in the line-out they gave you twenty lashes.

To stop off for a meal on a long away trip was unheard of because the club quite simply couldn't afford it. We players and the club officials took our own sandwiches on away trips. For years I thought knives and forks were jewellery.

Poor relations? One Monday night my team-mate Dave Trick arrived at the club feeling very sluggish and out of sorts. He said he was constipated and asked if anyone had anything to relieve his problem. 'Go and sit on the loo and I'll come and read you ghost stories. It's the best we can do,' Roger Spurrell told him.

Bath may not have had much money but many of the players

themselves had even less. In 1977 I wandered around with two 10p pieces in my trouser pocket hoping they'd mate.

The life of a Bath player was highly enjoyable but far from glamorous. In 1978 we played at London Irish and after the game Dave Trick, who was at the time still a student at Bath University, and I, 'resting between jobs', sat making the one pint each we could afford last the four hours before we were due to board the coach for the journey home.

The Bath officials and senior players would never let those on 'tight budgets' go without a beer, but after that particular game Dave and I were feeling somewhat self-conscious about accepting drinks from our team-mates and friends when we didn't have the money to reciprocate.

'I've got an idea to get us another pint each,' said Dave as we sat together in London Irish lounge bar. He took me over to where the broadcaster and thriller writer Kevin Columba Fitzgerald, a former player of the 1920s and 1930s and at the time a committee member at London Irish, was standing. Fitzgerald always liked to have his opinion sought on any subject and, as we stood near him, Dave and I pretended to be having a friendly argument about, of all things, imperial measurements.

'No, no, no! I'm telling you you're wrong, Coochie!' said Dave, raising his voice to catch Fitzgerald's attention.

'And I say I'm right!' I retorted.

Dave looked up as if Fitzgerald had suddenly caught his eye. 'Excuse me, Mr Fitzgerald,' he said. 'Could you settle this argument for us?'

'Try me,' said Fitzgerald, a lovely man but a famous know-all.

'Gareth and I have been having a friendly argument,' explained Dave. 'He says a gill is four pints – that is, half a gallon – and I keep trying to tell him it's not. A gill is two pints, a quarter of a gallon. Which is it?'

You'd have thought Dave had asked Fitzgerald his opinion of Einstein's Theory of Relativity the degree of consideration he gave the question before answering. 'You are right, young man,' Fitzgerald said at last, pointing to Dave and puffing himself out like a peacock. 'A gill is two pints, one quarter of a gallon.'

I affected not to be convinced as Dave and I thanked Fitzgerald for his time and sidled over to the bar. Dave caught the attention of the London Irish club steward behind the bar and ordered two pints of best bitter. 'Can you put them on Mr Fitzgerald's tab?' he said nonchalantly as the steward asked for the money. The barman looked very dubious indeed.

Dave turned away from the bar and raised an arm to catch the attention of Kevin Fitzgerald. 'You did say two pints, Mr Fitzgerald?' he called.

'Yes, two pints,' Kevin Fitzgerald nodded, and the steward duly added the drinks to his tab.

Now, before we get accused of pulling a fast one at the expense of the Irish, let me say that Dave pulled this trick with me at several English clubs as well. A downright devious act of chicanery, I know. On leaving university Dave went on to become a lawyer. I rest my case.

3

Wails From Wales

I BECAME a man within eighty minutes.

At eighteen years of age I was pitched into the Bath first team and in my second game I found myself playing at Pontypool against that famous front row of Graham Price, Bobby Windsor and Charlie Faulkner.

I went out on to that field a boy and came back a man. A battered and bleeding, crying man, but a man none the less. I had thought of myself as a young hard case until I played against the three most imposing forwards Welsh, and probably British, rugby has ever produced. They threw me around like a rag doll and in the scrums I was pushed back so far and so quickly you'd have thought I was trying to scrummage against a Chieftain tank. With hindsight I think I would have preferred a Chieftain tank. At least it wouldn't have taken the piss as it rolled over the top of me.

'Look you, boys, here's a nice new Bath shirt to clean our boots on,' Pricey said every time the three of them trampled all over me.

As no-side sounded, the players of both teams shook hands. Graham, Bobby and Charlie made a big show of checking their boots as they came off the field. 'Won't have to clean them tonight, Bobby,' said Pricey, studying his clean boots, then looking over at me. 'You can come here again, boyo. You could make doormats a thing of the past.'

As the years passed and that wonderful front row got older, I too grew wiser. Eventually, as I became more experienced, I gained the upper hand on those three rascals. But it was a good few years on, I can tell you.

Following Pontypool my next two games were away to Llanelli and Cardiff. As an eighteen-year-old I could have asked for an easier baptism but Genghis Khan's armies had long since been disbanded.

In the seventies English sides shied away from playing teams from Wales because they knew they'd be in for a hard time and certain defeat. Jack Rowell saw things differently. On taking over as coach he told the players he wanted to make Bath the greatest club side in Great Britain. He wanted us to cut our teeth on games against Welsh clubs. Jack's theory was that if we learned from each game and became fitter and technically better than the Welsh teams, who were streets ahead of English clubs at the time, there would come a day when Bath would become a great side.

Those early games were hard for us. We thought it a moral victory if we came away from Wales having lost by only fifteen or twenty points. When it came to playing English teams, however, we found it relatively easy. We started to record handsome victories against the Saracens and Wasps of this world and, in time, our much-improved fitness and technical prowess, combined with Jack Rowell's ability to add quality players to the team, enabled us to gain the upper hand against Welsh teams. Jack's plan worked well and today it is the Bath second XV that plays Pontypool and beats them regularly.

I encountered many characters on those trips to Wales but the biggest and most enigmatic was Charlie Faulkner, part of that legendary Pontypool front row. No one knew for sure how old Charlie was. When he was picked for the first of his nineteen caps for Wales in their 25–10 victory over France at the Parc des Princes in 1975, the Welsh selectors inquired at Pontypool about Charlie's age. The club had no official record and, when then they asked Charlie, he told them he was twenty-six. In fact he was thirty-four. So Charlie, unbeknownst to anybody, started his international career at an age when many players are thinking about retirement.

Charlie was finally rumbled when Pontypool toured Japan in 1979. Prior to the tour all the players were told to hand in their passports to the management. Charlie's year of birth, 1941, was, of course, there in black ink on his passport but before handing it over he had the foresight to change the one to a nine. He might have got clean away with it if he hadn't used a red pen.

I'm often asked which is the greatest rugby side I have ever seen or played against, and my answer is always the same: that wonderful Wales team of the mid-to late seventies. It is a mark of any great sportsman that he is known simply by his nickname or initials – Pele, Bestie, Both, Lester. To this day we still refer to members of that great Welsh side as J.P.R., J.J., Merv the Swerve and Pricey. During this period Wales were untouchable. They won the Five Nations Championship outright four times between 1975 and 1979, a remarkable achievement which included two Grand Slams (defeating the other four competing nations – England, Scotland, Ireland and France), in 1976 and 1978. This unprecedented sequence of success included four successive Triple Crowns (beating the other three home countries – Ireland having a united team), from 1976 to 1979.

The home of Welsh national rugby, Cardiff Arms Park, was a graveyard for opposition teams. For fourteen years, from 1968 until 1982, when Scotland won 34–18, Wales remained unbeaten at home.

Unfortunately for Welsh rugby, the players in this marvellous side were allowed to grow old together when they should have been gradually replaced by younger men. Many of them, including Gareth Edwards, J.P.R. Williams, Mervyn Davies, Derek Quinnell, Bobby Windsor and Gerald Davies, retired around the same time. It proved to be a massive blow to Welsh rugby and it took them years to recover from it.

What is more, the administrators of the game in Wales had become very complacent. They had wallowed in the success of that tremendous national side and did little to develop rugby at grass-roots level in the Principality. Welsh RU officials believed that the great players would just keep emerging. It didn't happen. Welsh rugby had set a high standard to which all other countries aspired but, while Wales stood still, the world had not only caught up, it had overtaken them.

When Wales lost 16–13 in Cardiff to Western Samoa in the 1991 World Cup and 26–24 to Canada in 1993, it was obvious that a whole generation of quality rugby players had been lost. These results really jolted the Welsh RU. They decided something drastic had to be done, and quickly. Now good progress has been made to develop rugby in the towns and valleys. Mini-rugby and schools of excellence are springing up all over the Principality, and young players of both sexes are receiving quality coaching and learning good habits. This, together with the emergence in the national team of players such as Rupert Moon, Wayne Proctor, David Manley and Steve Williams, should ensure that Welsh rugby will emerge once again as a real force at world level.

Another influencing factor in the decline of Welsh rugby was the fragmentation of local communities. It is no coincidence that the players of that great team of the seventies all came from close-knit communities situated in an area spanning about 24 miles by 65 miles, from Llanelli in the west to Newport in the east, Cardiff and Swansea in the south, and Pontypool in the north – a very small part of a country that is not itself large.

The effect was that the region produced players who knew one another inside out. There was a strong sense of togetherness and brotherhood which paid handsome dividends. When Wales were in a tight corner or the chips were down, those players would encourage and battle for one another. They were like one large family and it made them hellishly difficult to play against. Proof of that bond is that even today those players are still the best of pals.

Coinciding with the lack of development of Welsh rugby at grass-roots level came the decline of the traditional industries such as coal and steel. People left their close communities in search of alternative employment. The people of South Wales lost not only their jobs but also the close ties of their community life. It showed on the rugby pitch.

The Welsh team that competed in the 1991 World Cup had a disjointed look about it. When they found themselves under the cosh against Western Samoa in one of their group matches, they showed a distinct lack of togetherness and in the end they simply capitulated. The Phil Bennetts, Gareth Edwardses and Bobby Windsors of this world would never have done that in a million years.

To return to Charlie Faulkner, he and Ray Gravell, who was a bulldozer of a centre from Llanelli, were walking off the Cardiff practice pitch in the spring of 1978 before Wales left for a tour of Australia.

As they made their way to the dressing rooms, Ray walked through a patch of grass thick with buttercups. 'You shouldn't have done that,' Charlie told Ray. 'You've trampled down all those buttercups. It means you'll never have butter again in your life.'

Ray simply laughed, but Charlie was adamant. 'My mother

told me that. She also said that if you hurt a honey bee you'll never have honey again, either.'

Ray dismissed Charlie's old wives' tales and the pair showered before going into the Members' Bar for a thirst-quencher. As they walked in the barmaid was crouching down and sweeping something off the floor with a dustpan and brush. It was clear from her shudders and exclamations of disgust that she had found something extremely distasteful.

'What's up, love?' Charlie asked as he eased himself on to a barstool and peered over the counter.

'A cockroach came out from behind those crates of soft drinks,' the barmaid said. 'But I killed it.'

Ray Gravell took his place on another barstool and turned to Charlie. 'Are you going to tell her, Charlie, or should I?'

4

Hell on at St Helens

THE HAMMERINGS Bath took at the hands of Welsh clubs in the early days under Jack Rowell were all part of a learning curve which would eventually lead to us becoming the most successful English club side ever. The five Courage League Championships and nine cups won are a remarkable achievement, especially when one considers that those trophies have been won at a time when the standard of English club rugby has been at its highest and certainly its most competitive.

In 1976–7 Bath travelled to Swansea, more in hope than anything else. Swansea were an exceptionally strong side which, in Mervyn Davies, Geoff Wheel, Roger Blyth, Peter Llewellyn and Barry Clegg, had players of international class.

These were the days when the only fast food was stewed prunes and the only things that came ready to serve were tennis balls. It was also an era in which Bath did not have the forwards to gain the upper hand over the leading English clubs, let alone one of the strongest sides in Wales.

One of our forwards, a postman, was Brian Jenkins, a great character with a wonderful sense of humour. Brian once told me that on his delivery round in Bath was someone who was taking a correspondence course to become a stand-up comedian. Brian knew this from the publicity blurb printed on the envelope he delivered from the course, which said, 'Be a top-class comedian in twenty easy lessons.'

On the coach to Swansea I was sitting next to Brian and just by way of conversation I asked if he knew how the recipient of the comedians' correspondence course was getting on.

'I only delivered the first three instalments,' he said.

'What happened to the rest?' I asked.

'Well, put it this way,' replied Brian, turning towards me with a cheeky grin. 'I'm opening at the Palladium next week.'

Brian used to be ribbed something rotten on those away trips. The players would read newspapers to pass the journey and one or two, like myself or Richard Hill, would also have a go at the crosswords. When you were stuck you simply shouted out the clue in the hope that someone could provide the answer.

'Overworked postman?' I shouted during one away journey.

'How many letters?' asked Brian, rising to the bait.

'Thousands and thousands!' Richard and I chorused.

Apart from his wonderful sense of humour, Brian's other obvious characteristic was his nervousness. He had a twitch that made him jerk his head to one side while the left side of his mouth twitched upwards and his left eye winked. Fortunately this was not constant, merely a reaction that came to the fore in times of stress or excitement.

As we ran out on to the St Helens pitch, little did we know that Swansea's giant forward Geoff Wheel, one of the hardest men in Wales, suffered from a similar affliction. As luck would have it, neither Geoff nor his Swansea team-mates were aware of Brian's nervous twitch, either. Five minutes into the game the first line-out occurred. As the forwards lined up alongside one another, Brian found himself next to Big Geoff. The occasion started to get to Brian and, because he was anxious about winning line-out ball against such a formidable opponent, his tic started up involuntarily.

Geoff Wheel turned to see Brian staring at him, twitching away like mad. Geoff's face turned the colour of a Welsh international jersey. The veins in his temples stood out like Biros as he glared at the man who, it seemed, had the temerity to make fun of his affliction.

Brian, not insensitive, realised that all was not well with Big Geoff and, not knowing the reason for the Welsh giant's anger, tried a smile to placate him. Unfortunately for Brian, this smile was immediately followed by an almighty heaving twitch. It was like throwing petrol on a fire.

As the ball was fed into the line Geoff Wheel wound back a fist the size of a ham shank. As the full force of his punch connected with Brian's jaw, the noise was heard in the dugouts on the far side of the field.

Brian took off like a cowboy being thrown through a saloon's swing doors. Brian was, if anything, a tough cookie himself and, scrambling to his feet, he went for Geoff's throat with both hands.

'Cut it out! What's up with you two?' Swansea's Roger Blyth shouted as Brian and Geoff were pulled apart by their respective team-mates.

Order restored, the game got underway once again and for ten minutes or so all seemed well – until the next line-out was called. Brian took his position alongside Geoff. Just as the ball was fed into the line, Brian gave a sideways glance to check the position Geoff had taken. As he did so, Geoff checked on Brian. As the two faces met, Brian's nerves got the better of him again.

The twitching Geoff Wheel forgot the ball and, fists flying, launched himself at the unsuspecting Brian. Toe to toe they slugged it out until once again the referee and players pulled the snarling pair apart. 'For God's sake, what is it with you two?' asked the Swansea legend Mervyn Davies.

'He started it!' Big Geoff shouted, pointing an accusing finger at Brian.

'Like hell I did. It was him! I did nothing,' said Brian.

The game resumed, only to be halted again some fifteen minutes later as Bath's John Horton called referee Bryn Jones' attention to an off-the-ball incident. They were at it again. Big Geoff was laying into Brian and the red mist of anger had come down like a curtain across his eyes. It took no fewer than five Swansea players to pull him away.

'Tell him to stop!' Geoff screamed convulsively at the referee.

'Stop what? It's him! He's bloody mental,' a battered and bruised Brian shouted back.

Referee Jones called over the two captains, Jim Waterman and Mervyn Davies. 'I don't know what's going on between those two, but I want you to tell them that if there is any more of it they're both off.'

With their respective captains now also laying down the law, Brian and Geoff both settled down to playing rugby – for all of five minutes.

Brian's inadvertent twitching had by now reduced Big Geoff's mental stability to that of a drug-crazed psycho whose Giro is late. As he once more threw a barrage of punches, even we players were getting tired of their private battle and were calling for the referee to dismiss them both so that we could get on with playing rugby.

They stood facing one another, Jim Waterman and myself holding back Brian; Roger Blyth and Barry Clegg restraining big Geoff. It was then that, simultaneously, both of them twitched. Jim and I tightened our grip on Brian whilst the Swansea lads did the same with Big Geoff.

'There! See? He's been mocking me all game like that!' said Geoff through gritted teeth.

'Me? It's you who's been doing it to me!' retorted Brian.

Our prop, Bertie Meddick, stepped between the snarling pair. 'You bloody goons,' he said, hands on hips and offering them one of his icy stares. 'Nobody is taking the piss. You've *both* got twitches! Now, can we get on with the damn game?'

The private feud between Brian and Geoff had a humorous aspect to it. But it does illustrate how difficult it is for a referee to spot off-the-ball altercations. The ball is the hub of the game and the referee must have his eye on it at all times so that he can award offside, forward passes and the like.

It is little wonder that skirmishes 20 yards from the ball go unnoticed. Before 1994, when the law was changed, touch-judges had the power to intervene in international matches but not at club level. As we saw in that year when the touring South Africans played Neath, private battles can go unchecked. That night the trouble was not nipped in the bud and the problem escalated, and what happened in the end was a disgrace to rugby. Hard, physical play is one thing but out-and-out violence has no place in the game. If the touch-judges had been more experienced in the prompting of referees, the thuggery at Neath might not have happened. The law relating to this was changed in 1994 to allow touch-judges to bring incidents to the referee's attention. To my mind it was a change for the better and, as time passes, touch-judges are becoming more adept at spotting incidents on the blind side of a referee.

Considering the pummelling Geoff Wheel gave Brian that day, it's a wonder he didn't suffer brain damage. Fortunately he was all right and after the game, which we lost 30–12, the two made up and apologies flowed almost as abundantly as the beer.

The Growth of Bath

'Don't ask me about emotion in a Welsh dressing room. I cry when I watch Little House on the Prairie.'

Bob Norster, Cardiff, Wales and British Lions.

'Gareth would fight tooth and nail for any club he were to play for. But he'd die for Bath.'

Richard Hill, Bath, England and British Lions.

5

Gaining Experience

A s a nineteen-year-old in 1977, I was what Jack Rowell jokingly referred to as 'Green around the gills and a stranger to the lavatory.'

The year before, I had had a tough baptism in the first XV at Bath and was struggling to find my feet. Fortunately Mike Fry, a stalwart of our local arch-rivals Bristol, took me under his wing and offered advice.

Mike is one of the nicest guys you could ever wish to meet. He is also one of the hardest. Not the tallest of props, Mike made up for the inches he lacked with great strength and determination. In many ways he was a mentor because, as the years went by, I too relied on those two attributes to compensate for the fact that I don't look like someone who fell asleep in a greenhouse when young.

Mike was what I would call a 'physical player'. There were times when, like me later, he would become embroiled in a 'physical debate' with a member of the opposition. Mike could dish it out but, by the same token, he never complained when someone gave it back to him.

To watch my tutor in action, in 1977 I went along to a midweek game between Bristol and Bridgend at the Brewery Field. During the match Bridgend's Welsh international centre

Steve Fenwick and Mike crossed one another. At one point in the second half, off the ball, Mike caught Steve with an upper-cut to the jaw of which Mike Tyson would have been proud. 'You're a dirty bastard, Fry,' Steve said, literally taking it on the chin.

'Yeah,' said Mike, 'and don't any of you Bridgend boys ever forget it!'

Ten minutes later Mike emerged from a scrum, mouth pouring with blood and minus two teeth.

'You live by the sword, die by the sword in this game, Pup,' Mike said to me afterwards through swollen lips, using the nickname he had coined for me. 'Never forget this. People will watch and admire a skilful player. But if you're skilful and physical, they'll bloody well listen to you as well.'

As a prop Mike had considerable skill, and at that stage of my rugby development it was what I lacked. He was coming towards the end of his career and, as someone starting out on mine, I was to learn much from him.

A few years on I was the pack leader in the Somerset county side. One or two of the Somerset County RFU officials thought I was 'too aggressive' and 'not the calibre of chap' they wanted to see representing their team. They dropped me. Who did they replace me with? Mike Fry!

After ten minutes of a match against Lancashire during which Mike pasted two lads into the advertising hoardings and tried to take Bill Beaumont's ears home for ashtrays, the county selectors must have been left thinking I was quite genteel and mild-mannered in comparison. Mike was really wound up for that game, so much so that when he left the Somerset dressing room, he didn't bother to open the door first. The selectors found it half-way up the tunnel. I might be mistaken but I don't think Mike was picked for the county again.

Bath were in a very fluctuating state at this time as Jack Rowell and our captain, Jim Waterman, brought in new players and let go those who did not figure in their plans. Partly due to this, and partly because of Jack's insistence that we competed against the top Welsh clubs as part of our development, our results swung like a pendulum. One week we would win by thirty points, only to lose by the same margin the following week. The Bath team of the late seventies could have had a disjointed feel and look to it in view of all the changes that were taking place, but one of the major things that helped bond us as a family was Jack Rowell's insistence that we toured in the close season.

At the time neither Bath as a club, nor any of the players for that matter, had much in the way of money, as I've said. Nevertheless, we embarked upon our first tours, albeit on the cheap. There were no five-star hotels for Bath players in those days. In fact, there were no hotels. If, for example, we played four games in northern France, we tried to arrange for each player or official to stay with his opposite number, on the promise that if our hosts ever came to Bath on tour, we would reciprocate, which we often did.

Of course, there were times when this was not possible, for example, when a tour involved travelling great distances between cities or towns in a country like Canada. I slept in the back of a van in Amsterdam, on a mattress in a garage in Montreal and occupied one of twenty or so sleeping bags that were laid out in one long row inside a wind tunnel used for testing aircraft in Seattle. The wind tunnel wasn't turned on, of course, but with twenty rugby players sleeping off a curry and about seven pints of beer apiece, it might as well have been.

Bath must somehow have found some money for touring because I don't ever recall any of us players having to put our hands in our pockets to buy a drink. Although the tours were very much a shoestring job, for some it was their first time abroad, and many of us were visiting countries and places we had never before experienced, so we loved every minute of it. If it meant sleeping on a garage floor to play against Ottawa and marvel at Lake Ontario or the Niagara Falls, then I was perfectly happy to do it.

Canada was one of the very first tours we embarked upon. For a start I had never flown such a long distance before and was a bit nervous, but I soon relaxed into the happy touring atmosphere. The stewardess came up to John Horton and asked if he would like cotton wool or a boiled sweet to combat the pressure differential on take-off. 'I'll have the cotton wool,' said John. 'I tried the boiled sweets last time but they just kept falling out of my ears.'

It set the humorous tone for a tour that would turn us into a happy bunch who really got to know one another well. As a result as individuals we were willing to fight to the death for each other. It was an attribute Jack Rowell was to instil into every successive Bath side and one that would play a significant part in all future success.

One of the marvellous things about playing rugby is that your team-mates come from all walks of life. It hadn't been that long since I'd been hanging around street corners associating with petty criminals, but on those tours I found myself sitting next to other players whose jobs ranged from labourer to marketing executive, farmer, lawyer and policeman.

During the Canadian tour we were guests of a club in Penticton. On one of our free days I found myself out on the town with Simon Jones, a business executive, John Horton, a master at Kingswood Public School in Bath and Dave Trick, a solicitor. We had found our way to a very dubious bar called Slack Alice's. It was not the cleanest of places – in fact there was so much dirt on the tables the only way a fly could have walked across them have would been on stilts. The loos were up a narrow flight of stairs that had so many cobwebs John said they looked as if they had been backcombed. To call it a bar is a bit of a misnomer because it was actually a twenty-four-hour strip joint.

We settled at a table and we're enjoying our first drink, a Labatt's, when Simon asked me what my ambition was in life. 'I think I want to get into marketing or sporting promotion,' I replied in all sincerity. 'What's yours?'

'Another Labatt's with a whisky chaser, seeing as you're asking,' said Simon, polishing off what remained of his first beer.

There endeth my first lesson.

Five hours later the table was holding us up. Dave Trick and I were legless, he worse than I. We were both staying at the home of Mike and Weston McCauley who played full-back and outside-half respectively for Penticton. To this day I cannot remember how we managed to find our way back from Slack Alice's to the McCauleys' home, except that for the best part of the journey Dave was so far gone I had to carry him.

Our hosts had given us a lovely bedroom to share that boasted the rarity, for the time, of an en-suite bathroom. Not wanting to disturb the McCauleys, who had been kind and generous in their hospitality, I stealthily found my way to our room, still carrying Dave. I closed the door quietly behind me and propped Dave against it whilst I sat on the bed and emptied the change from my pockets on to the bedside table and took off my shoes.

Poor Dave was in such a terrible state that I decided to undress him and put him to bed, but he wasn't having any of it. He shrugged me away with a dismissive wave of his right hand and lurched forward into the bathroom.

I took off my clothes, flopped into bed and was asleep almost immediately. I think I'd been dead to the world for some twenty minutes or so when I was suddenly awoken by the sound of banging and hissing. Drunk as I was, the loud banging made me jump from the bed with a start.

It took me a few moments to collect myself and to realise that the banging was coming from the en-suite. On opening the door, I was taken aback by the sight of Dave Trick standing inside the perspex-panelled shower cubicle. The shower was on and he was fully clothed, banging on the cubicle door. Afraid he would awaken our hosts, I yanked the door open. A totally soaked and forlorn Dave looked up from his sodden shoes.

'Thank God!' he whimpered in relief. 'It's been pissing down out here for half an hour and I can't find my key!'

6

Rocky Mountain Way

FRASER VALLEY is a small town in the Canadian Rockies with spectacular views in each and every direction. It is so small that it was rumoured that the local fire brigade was a four-year-old bed-wetter and the mayor and town idiot one and the same person.

During the Bath tour of 1978 their rugby club also gave us one of the most physical games in which I have ever been involved. Fraser Valley, as I say, is small – if you drove down its one street at 50mph and blinked you'd probably miss it. Little wonder, then, that it could not muster a rugby team from its inhabitants. Instead they recruited from the lumberjack camps up in the mountains.

These lumberjacks, we were told, trained up there, spending months in the forests without the company of women or any home comforts. For relaxation they competed with one another in a game that involved throwing tree trunks over marked distances. Let's not beat about the bush – or even forest – we're talking mean men.

The Canadians play a really physical game. After a season of being battered by top Welsh club sides, what better way to wind down than to face a team whose smallest player was 6ft 1in with shoulders like bags of coal?

In retrospect, this was the start of the toughening process that was to take Bath to the very top in club rugby and keep us there for well over a decade. In games against the Welsh it wasn't unusual for someone from the second row to send a punch up into the hooker's face. In fact, it was so common that we began to expect it on our trips to Wales and the referees didn't even bother to pull anyone up for it. As a teenager in the side I was learning quickly that, if I was going to survive, I'd have to scrap and fight every inch of the way, seeing as I wasn't exactly blessed with an abundance of skill.

One of the intimidating tactics of the day, though one does not see it so much now, was for the opposition to try to bend you in two in the scrum by pushing you down until you were literally bent double. This goes some way to explaining why, on my retirement in 1994, the Bath club doctor told me I had the physical fitness of a twenty-five-year-old but the back of an octogenarian.

Fraser Valley were happy to adopt this ruse and worse. Where pure rugby was concerned, the result should have been 60–0 in our favour. As it was, the scores were level when the game ended. There were still twenty minutes to go, mind you, but referee Michael Fuller had had enough. The fighting had been so bad that Mr Fuller had obviously come to the conclusion that, should one team eventually lose, the next logical step would be murder.

The fact that the second half lasted only twenty minutes came as a relief to Nick Maslen. He had spent an hour of purgatory battling against his opposite number in the back of the line-out. His opponent, a man by the name of Sanchez, turned out to be the Panamanian national 85kg wrestling champion and former amateur heavyweight boxing champion of Central America. This guy obviously harboured thoughts of regaining the boxing title because throughout the game he was determined to get in a little practice by using Nick's head as a punchbag.

After the game we all repaired to the one bar in town to down the drink of that trip, which we christened a B52. Actually it should have been called the ironing-board cocktail because after one your legs were ready to fold under you. It was a sophisticated little drink, comprising a shot of everything from the optics and the top shelf in one large glass. Nick Maslen took three sips of his and within minutes was walking and talking like John Inman.

Roger Spurrell, who had recently been appointed captain, said that after the battering to which Nick had been subjected, a B52 was bad news on an empty stomach, so eight of us went down to the Fraser Valley diner for steak and chips.

As we sat down at one long table we marvelled at the size of the plates that were placed before us. Each one could have provided work for a Stoke-on-Trent pottery for about three months and it would have taken a kiln the size of the London Planetarium to fire them. When the steaks arrived, our jaws dropped. 'I've got half a cow here!' Roger exclaimed. Indeed, we all had.

As we were all so strapped for cash in those days we were worried that we wouldn't be able foot the bill for such a gigantic meal. At the end Nick Maslen had recovered enough sense to try to avoid the bill by attempting to lock himself in the loo. Unfortunately for him the rest of us wouldn't let him in.

Those steaks apart, what spurred us on in those days was hunger. A hunger for success. The more we travelled together, the closer we became as a unit and the more we got to understand just what Jack Rowell wanted from us. 'A close team plays well together,' Jack used to say. When in later years we achieved the success we all wanted for Bath, one of the things that ensured we remained hungry was touring. As a successful team we had brought money into Bath RFC, which enabled us to persuade the committee to fund tours to exotic places such as the Far East or Australia, where we stayed in top-class hotels, not on garage floors. Having tasted this lifestyle we wanted to sample more of it, and to do that we had to keep on winning. As Roger Spurrell once said, 'We want Bath to be to rugby what Manchester United are to soccer.'

Towards the end of the Canadian tour we stopped off to play a game against Sault Saint Marie, which nestles between Lake Superior and Lake Huron. We were staying in a youth hostel that looked out across to the USA, where on a clear day you could see part of the state of Michigan.

Having won our game earlier in the day, we players were given a night to spend as we pleased. Our youth hostel was on the outskirts of Sault Saint Marie and Roger Spurrell, John Horton, John Palmer, Dave Trick and myself decided against catching a taxi into the city for a night out. Although it was against house rules, the five of us decided to chip in a few dollars apiece to buy as much beer and food as we could from the local provisions store and have our own surreptitious session in the boiler room of the hostel.

It was decided that John Palmer and John Horton would get themselves off to the store to buy as much as they could from the kitty, while Dave and I sneaked chairs from upstairs down to the boiler room and Roger kept a look-out for the hostel management.

The chairs in place, Roger spotted the two Johns struggling across the hostel car park with their booty. Opening the side door, he beckoned them inside. 'OK, boys, let's see what our money managed to buy.'

The two Johns dropped their heavy load in the middle of the boiler-room floor. There were two crates of beer, two crates of Guinness and three bags of crisps.

Roger, who, like the rest of us, had not eaten after the game, stared blankly at it all. Eventually he spoke. 'Why the hell did you have to go and buy all that food?'

7

The Team That Jack Built

PIETRO MASCAGNI, the Italian composer, so the story goes, was getting very irritated by an organ grinder who stood outside his home playing tunes from his opera *Cavalleria Rusticana* at about half the correct speed. Eventually the composer could stand it no longer and went outside to give the organ grinder a hard time, though he had a grudging admiration for the man for having chosen for his street organ tunes from *Rusticana* from all those available.

'I am Mascagni. Let me show you how to play this music properly so that you will become a successful organ grinder and really know how to entertain people,' Mascagni said, giving the handle of the hurdy-gurdy some vigorous turns.

The following day Mascagni again heard the organ grinder in the street outside and was pleased to hear his tunes being played correctly. When he looked out, he noticed a sign over the organ which said, 'Pupil of Mascagni'.

In many ways that anecdote has a parallel in the relationship between Jack Rowell and me. When we started our careers at Bath on the very same day, I was a raw, callow youth with little in the way of rugby skills. There were periods when he gave me a really hard time but I always felt he had admiration and respect for me, as I did for him. When Jack left Bath in 1994 to take over the reins of the England team, he said goodbye to an England international and British Lion. I was very much a 'pupil of Rowell'.

Jack is very good at managing businesses and he is also very good at managing rugby teams. He has the uncanny knack of being able to produce a winning side. He knows when players have to be replaced and possesses the ability to bring in one top-class performer for another. Not easy.

The wonderful thing about rugby is that no matter what standard of player you are, there is a club and level for you. Those Bath players who, in 1977, were content to amble through training and on Saturdays have one eye on the post-match socialising found themselves looking for that club.

Jack's office in the early days was tiny. The club employed a secretary to pop in once a week to type his correspondence. 'If that office were an inch smaller, it would constitute adultery,' Jack used to say when he and the secretary were in there together.

From his humble office he set about creating a team worthy of challenging the best rugby had to offer. He saw that in Mike Beese, Jim Waterman and Derek Wilde, Bath had good threequarters. He then promoted me from the United side and put me in the front row. Then, to everyone's amazement, he produced a recruit from Bristol who, on first sight, you would never have thought could be a rugby player. He was Derek Barry, a spindly lad with arms and legs like Biros.

'Last time I saw legs like that, they had a message tied to them,' John Palmer remarked on seeing him for the first time.

In the winter Derek used to arrive at the ground wearing a long, light grey overcoat. 'The pipe-cleaner's here,' I'd say, looking out of the dressing-room window.

Yet for all his litheness, Derek turned out to be a sturdy lad who could really play. In the line-out he surprised us all by outjumping everyone.

Jack set about building a good back row. Paul Simpson, another Geordie, came to the south-west with a Barbarians tour. Jack knew of Paul's ability from his own days in the north-east with Newcastle Gosforth and approached him. Paul never returned to the north. It helped that during the short tour with the Barbarians he met a Bristol girl. They are now happily married and have a lovely family. Jon Hall came up through the Spartans and Bath United sides before getting his chance with the first XV. He took it. From modest beginnings Jack had created a good back row that had the ability to win the ball.

At first we were erratic in our performances, and of course there were the trips across the border to play top Welsh teams as part of our 'toughening-up' programme. Gradually we started to win more often than we lost, an improvement that was reflected in the attendances at the Rec.

The joke about the Bath fan saying cheerio to the supporter nearest him and having to shout 'Goodbye' at the top of his voice to a guy at the far end of the ground was a thing of the past. A few hundred became 600, 1,000, then 2,000. Now, as I said earlier, attendances vary between 4,000 and 6,000 for home games.

People started to take us very seriously. The commercial side of the club began to take off and there was a general buzz about the place, as if everyone from chairman and committee to players and supporters knew we were part of something very special.

As players, we took on an attitude – the Welsh attitude, that of the players of the best club rugby there was then. Because of the heavy-duty encounters we'd had across the border, when we went to places such as Harlequins or Saracens, we found it wasn't as hard as playing Cardiff or Llanelli on a January night so cold that the local pawnbroker had to cover up his sign.

As a team we learned not only on-field skills from the

Welsh but also how to run a rugby club properly from top to bottom; how to look after our supporters. When we first went to play the Ebbw Vales and Pontypools of this world, we found we were not just taking on their rugby teams but the whole community as well. The Welsh lads gave their all for their particular town. It gave them a very hard edge indeed and a great sense of pride. When they had you back-pedalling they never let up. We could be trailing by thirty points but they'd never let us off the ropes. They'd continue to hammer away at us until they were forty or even fifty points ahead – the only time they stopped was when they heard the final whistle. It was this killer instinct that Jack instilled into every Bath player.

Rugby players can have fitness, skill and stamina but if they haven't got the right mental attitude they won't win trophies. The community attitude and the killer attitude were what we adopted. Jack preached this constantly and the likes of myself, Robbie Lye, Roger Spurrell, Richard Lee and Jack Foster practised it to the letter. We all wanted to become winners and fight tooth and nail for Bath and every ball. The dedication and commitment we developed were personified by Bertie Meddick. Ten minutes before the end of his very last training session before retiring from rugby altogether, Bertie squared up to me following an argument about whether the ball had been fed straight into the scrum during a sevens game – and I was his best pal!

We realised that inner fitness was just as important as outer fitness. Like Miss Jean Brodie with her girls, Jack Rowell told his boys they were 'different and superior'. Seeing is believing – unless you happen to have been on the Rodney King jury – and, as the victories started to mount up, we really did believe no one could touch us.

To play for Bath you had to be Jack Rowell's type of player. I'll never forget Roger Spurrell joining us. Roger was a giant, blond ex-paratrooper from Cornwall whom Jack had been tracking for some weeks and wanted to sign for Bath. He felt Roger could add even more aggression and hardness to the side. Jack had invited Roger to attend a Monday training session and afterwards gave him an 'interview' in his office.

'Well, has Spurrell the necessary aggression?' asked John Horton as Jack joined us in the bar some time later.

'Without a doubt,' said Jack. 'He took a swing at me during the interview!'

Jack hadn't just created his first real side at Bath. Like the Welsh over the border, he had created a community. From the early eighties onwards, when any team played Bath, they took on everyone – players, committee, supporters, townsfolk and all.

8

Jobs for the Boys

R UGBY UNION is an amateur sport. I think it will change and I see nothing wrong in its best exponents, along with the players of every other sport in the world, being paid to display their skills. One of the reasons people pay to watch rugby, or indeed any other sport, is to see players do the things they cannot do themselves: Will Carling sprinting 40 yards and weaving in and out of opponents to go over in the corner for a try; Kyran Bracken receiving the ball from a scrum and finding Rory Underwood with a 30-yard reverse pass. Not many can do it. Fewer can do it in the red-hot atmosphere of a Five Nations game with a 16-stone Scot or Frenchman breathing down their necks. So why shouldn't the very best players in the world receive some sort of reward for their skills and application?

When you reach the top in rugby, you need an understanding boss. You need time off work to attend Five Nations Championship games for a start, as the squads gather on the Wednesday preceding a match. An England tour can last a month. If you are lucky enough to be picked for a British Lions tour, it can last up to three months, even if these happen only once every four years. In between Lions tours there is, of course, the World Cup, which also takes place every four years. If you are a member of a side that does well in the final stages you can, with an acclimatisation period, be away for nigh on two months. With that amount of time away from work, you need an employer who is a cross between Job, Mother Theresa and Bill McLaren.

I'd left school with no qualifications, as I said. I loved PE, enjoyed English and drama but was only really competent at woodwork. It stands to reason, then, that when my fellow pupils left school with eight or nine 'O' levels, I left Aston Park Comprehensive with two spirit levels. Now that rugby had given me an interest in life, I knew I had to find work that would allow me to play the game. In the beginning I did a ragbag assortment of work, in the main jobs you didn't mind losing. My first attempt at financing myself was as a petrol-pump attendant. Remember them?

One day an elderly lady in a large Rover came in with a flat tyre. She was very distressed, so I took her into the office, made her a cup of tea and told her to sit down and relax while I changed the wheel for her. I meant well, but at the time I didn't know that you should never put the jack under the sump. Having changed the tyre, I waved her off on her way. Ten minutes later the garage received a call asking for the recovery vehicle to be sent out to attend to an elderly lady's Rover.

It turned out that the bottom of the sump had cracked under the weight of the car. The oil had cascaded on to the road, she hadn't noticed and, empty of oil, the engine had seized.

The lady got herself into a terrible state wondering how she would pay for the damage. I couldn't stand to see her like that, so I owned up to my boss about what I had done. The garage ended up having to foot the bill. As I say, rugby players need very understanding employers!

My boss didn't sack me or deduct any money from my wages. He understood that I'd only been trying to help. Years later, in

1984, he phoned me before Bath's first-ever John Player Cup semi-final. We were playing local rivals Gloucester. Tickets were like gold dust and he'd been unable to get any. Was there any chance of one? I sent him four.

My natural physique once got me a job as a debt collector. I was only a callow youth, really, and took it up partly in the hope of meeting sultry housewives who would beckon me indoors and demand that I accept payment in kind. To callow youth add misguided dreamer.

I certainly met a lot of housewives, but none of them was what Thomas More called love's young dream. It was amazing how the excuses were always the same. In most cases the men in their lives had skipped and left them. With no maintenance they were left to bring up the children — and there were always children — as best they could.

One day, on a Taunton council estate, a woman of about twenty-three opened the door to me, holding a baby about eighteen months old whilst two small children clung to her dress.

She was expecting the emergency benefit officer as she had totally run out of money. The last person she wanted on her doorstep was a debt collector. As she stood explaining that she couldn't pay me anything yet again, the emergency benefit officer from Social Services arrived. The unfortunate woman signed some forms and was told that a Giro would be issued 'probably tomorrow'.

As the officer left, the young mother was crying and screaming that she didn't have a penny and there was no food in the house. What was she going to give her kids for meals?

Me, a debt collector? Someone has to do it, but not me. I ended up giving the woman a fiver on the condition that she used it to buy food. The moment I got back to the debt agency office I resigned.

I did a bit of night-club bouncing after that. At £20 a night it paid very well. It kept the wolf from the door and there wasn't a great deal of trouble to sort out. The funniest night I had was when a group of students from Bristol University turned up. University students invariably do not cause fights, even when they are full of lager. However, neither are they known for their dress sense, and the club where I worked did have dress rules.

That night I stopped these students because one of them was not wearing a tie. I explained that the house rules were that all men had to wear a jacket, shirt and tie. One of the friends of the under-dressed lad thought he had a tie in his car, so the two of them went back to the car park while I let the others into the club.

Five minutes later the first two returned and I was amazed to see the tieless bloke wearing a set of jump leads round his neck. 'What the hell is this?' I said, stopping him on the door.

'Oh, we couldn't find a tie in the car. But we found these jump leads and thought we could make a tie out of them.'

I was taken aback to say the least. Working the door gives you a hunch about people, though, and seeing that they seemed nice enough lads, I allowed them in. As the youth with the jump-lead tie paid his entrance money I took him to one side. 'I'm allowing you in,' I said, 'but don't start anything!'

I was also a lumberjack for a time before finding work laying pavements in Keynsham, between Bath and Bristol. I must have laid half the pavements in the town. At the start of every day's work, the contract foreman would always say the same thing to me and the rest of the layers. 'Remember, lads, when laying these paving stones, they must be spot on.'

One day we were visited by an inspector from Avon Council Highways who had with him an instrument that looked to all intents and purposes like a giant geometrical compass. The inspector told us that it acted as a sort of spirit level and could measure the margin of error in laying a paving stone to within 1mm.

'It would be no good to us,' one of the lads in our gang said. 'Our paving stones have to be spot on!'

Playing for a top-class rugby team such as Bath means you have to find a job that allows you at least two months off a year for touring. I was drifting from one job to another without settling down to the security of anything permanent. In my teens I wasn't too bothered, but once I reached my twenties, I began to think long and hard about what I should be doing with my life outside rugby.

I mentioned this to one or two people at Bath and was told to bide my time whilst they saw 'what could be done'. Fortunately for me, a very keen supporter of Bath, Malcolm Pearce, had a successful company called Johnson's Wholesale News. Malcolm is one of the nicest guys you could wish to meet and I'm not just saying that because he offered me a job in the company's security division. From then on, when people asked me what I did for a living I simply said: 'I work in the media.'

Malcolm loves Bath Rugby Club, Somerset Cricket Club and Bath Races. He helps players either by taking them on himself or by persuading his business friends to offer them gainful employment. He set up a new division of the company called Chauffeurlink, which provided an upmarket car-rental service – and I mean upmarket. The cheapest car in the fleet was a BMW. I eventually became managing director of the company, a position I retained until I became Bath's commercial manager and a member of the coaching staff and set up my own PR and promotions company.

In 1990 Bath had a fixture at Gloucester. Our team coach was barely out of the Bath car park when it broke down. A telephone call to the coach company failed to produce a replacement as they were all booked out.

'No problem,' I said. 'We'll pop across to Chauffeurlink and we'll travel in cars.'

We made an arresting and impressive sight as we all pulled on to the area reserved for players' cars in the Gloucester car park. There was a Lotus Esprit S.4, a Mercedes 500SEC, a Porsche 928 54 Auto, a Jaguar V12 XJS and a BMW 850i automatic.

After the game I was having my post-match meal in the Players' Dining Room when Gloucester's Mike Teague came and sat down next to me. 'Would Bath ever be interested in signing me?' he inquired surreptitiously.

'Might be,' I whispered.

'If they did, what are the chances of them fixing me up with a job?' he asked out of the corner of his mouth.

'But you've got a good job.'

'Not as good as the bloody ones they find for you lot,' said Mike. 'I've seen the cars you all arrived in today.'

9

I'm All Right Jack

I N BETWEEN the years of 1977, when Jack Rowell arrived in Bristol to be managing director of Lucas Ingredients and took over at Bath, and 1984, when we won our first major trophy by beating arch-rivals Bristol 10–9 at Twickenham to clinch the John Player Cup (as it was called then), we played some super rugby, gradually improving with each passing season. After the years of standing still the renaissance really got underway. There were changes both on and off the field, and the only thing that remained constant was Jack's thirst for success and the single-mindedness with which he pursued it. 'We must be winners,' he told us one night at training. 'There's no point in us working all the hours God sends, training three nights a week in freezing shit and sweating blood on a Saturday, if we're only going to come second.' We all agreed with him.

Jack has a public reputation for being very strong and ruthless. He is. There are many who think that he is an unsympathetic bastard. He is. I've even heard it said that Jack is 'a self-regarding, inscrutable Geordie bastard who will stop at nothing to get what he wants'. He is that as well. But he is also the best manager-coach I have ever had the honour to play for and a man capable of great sensitivity, honesty, warmth and humour. 'There's only one man allowed to say, "There is nothing wrong with defeat," and that's Nelson Mandela's chiropodist!' he used to tell us.

It is true that from the moment he arrived at Bath it was obvious Jack wanted success and there would be casualties along the way. He was prepared to dump people and tread on one or two toes, even to lose the odd friend in the process, in order to achieve that success.

Yet the strange thing about Jack's behaviour is that, although he *is* very strong and ruthless, he never tells a person to his face that he is out. Jack caused a right old stir when he dropped Nigel Redman for the 1989 Pilkington Cup final against Leicester. Jack preferred Damian Cronin to Nigel, who had played well in the earlier rounds, particularly in our 6–3 win over Gloucester in the semi-final.

When a player is dropped he is naturally upset and disappointed. If he were to say to his coach, 'It's OK, I'm not too bothered about being left out,' then the coach should drum him out of the club because it would show that the player's heart wasn't in it. Nigel wasn't upset. He was bloody livid. Naturally enough, he wanted to know why he was not in the team for the final, so he went to Jack on the Sunday before the match to ask why he'd been dropped.

'Not now, Nigel,' Jack told him. 'I have a team to prepare for next Saturday's final. See me at training tomorrow night.'

At the Monday-night training session, Jack was equally elusive. 'Not now,' he told Nigel. 'Please bear with me. We'll have a good chat about it on Wednesday night after training.'

'After training on Wednesday night, then?' Nigel reiterated.

'Yes,' said Jack. 'Definitely.'

We trained on the Wednesday under Jack's supervision and, as the session drew to a close, he called us into a group. 'Right, some running just to finish off, then you can go in for your shower,' he said.

At Lambridge the land the club owns extends beyond the pitches. Jack pointed to the river that runs along the far end of the training ground, beyond the pitches. 'I want you to run three-quarter pace all the way to the riverbank,' he instructed. 'When you reach it, turn and sprint all the way back here. Then straight in for your shower.'

Off we went. I had gone only 20 yards or so when I glanced back over my shoulder to see Jack running across one of the pitches to the car park. As I neared the far fence I glanced back again, just in time to see his car screeching off at top speed.

When we all got back into the dressing room, Nigel went off in search of Jack. 'You're wasting your time,' I called after him. 'He's gone home.'

Nigel stood, hands on hips, steam rising from his back, sweat pouring from his face. 'So that's why he had us running all the way down to the river – to give him time to make his getaway,' he fumed. 'I tell you, that bastard Rowell could wind up Mother Theresa so much she'd put her fist through a stained glass window!'

We beat Leicester 10–6 in that Cup final, so, as ever, I suppose Jack's team selection was justified.

Jack's first job when he was appointed England manager in 1994 was to take charge of the tour to South Africa. After winning the first Test, England lost the second. An insight into what sort of person Jack is is how he deals with failure. He sacked the England coach, Dick Best.

It came as no surprise to me. From the moment Jack was appointed I wondered just how long Dick would last. On that South Africa tour Jack took two coaches: Dick and Les Cusworth, who works very well with the manager. I remember thinking then that, for all his wonderful record, Dick's days were numbered. If it hadn't been that second Test it would have been something else, of that I'm certain. Defeat in that game gave Jack the excuse he wanted once the tour was over.

Jack is autocratic and I knew that, as well as being manager, he'd want to be in charge of the coaching of the England players. It means that the buck stops with him, but he knows that and thrives on it. Some people don't like that much responsibility and pressure. Jack does.

In South Africa he completely ignored Dick Best. One morning in a hotel lounge in Cape Town I saw Dick chatting to a reporter after the daily press conference.

'Same place, same time tomorrow?' asked the reporter.

'How should I know?' said Dick.

'Well, you're the England coach, aren't you?'

'No,' said Dick. 'I'm just a mushroom on this tour. Kept in the dark and living off Jack Rowell's bullshit!'

After the tour Jack went away on business. It was while he was uncontactable that Dick Best learned of his fate. Jack didn't tell him in person or even ring him. It's a tough life. Jack is very single-minded and puts himself on the line. If people are not of similar mind, then, as far as Jack is concerned, they have to go.

If, say, Andy Robinson, Richard Hill, Stuart Barnes, Simon Halliday or I had been on international duty with England and returned to Bath brimming with self-confidence, egos polished by the press after a victory, Jack would quickly bring us down to earth. 'It may be good enough for England but it isn't good enough for Bath!' he'd say when making us repeat a set-piece move again and again.

In 1984 Bath played Leicester away and Jack arranged for a video of the game to be made so that we could analyse it later in the week. We lost the match, and on the journey home, where the M69 links to the M6 near Coventry, the Bath team bus pulled into a pub so that we could test their bitter and Guinness. The landlord, unbeknown to us, had some weeks before had a bad time with a student rugby team who had become boisterous and unruly. As we entered the lounge bar he came up to us with his hands raised.

'Sorry, gentlemen. I don't allow rugby players in here no more.'

'These aren't rugby players,' said Jack, following us in. 'And I've got a bloody video here to prove it!'

Ch-Ch-Ch-Ch-Changes

'I've learned one thing. When the players
take over, they ruin everything.'

Kitch Christie, Springboks coach

'You ask me if Headquarters worry about
change. Well, hardly – everything is paid for
by cheque.'

RFU official on BBC Radio Sport

10

The Rugby Revolution

S INCE 1987 rugby has undergone a metamorphosis. More changes have taken place in the subsequent eight years than in the previous seventy. More will follow. It is still ostensibly an amateur sport, though that must change in the near future. Players may be classed as amateur but, make no mistake, top-flight rugby is now very big business indeed.

The period between 1987 and 1994 has become known as the 'rugby revolution'. The rapid developments on and off the field have seen a growth of interest and an upsurge in attendances. In 1980 Bath were pulling crowds of 700 to 800; now, as I've said, the average is around 5,000. It's not only at Bath that this is happening either; attendances are up at all the major clubs, while at grass-roots level the game is burgeoning.

As someone who has been happy to be part of the after-dinner-speaking circuit for a number of years, I have witnessed at first hand the growth of rugby at junior club level. Take the north-east, for example. This area has always loved its sport and the folk up there turn up in great numbers in support of their teams. By tradition the north-east has always been a soccer area, but in recent years the number of rugby clubs that have been springing up is phenomenal. Seaham, Seaton Carew, Wearside, Wallsend and Chester-le-Street are just five of the many which have been formed in the last few years. It seems that every north-eastern town or village now has a rugby team whereas before they were represented only by soccer and perhaps cricket.

What is more, when you visit these clubs, they're not running simply one team, but often six or seven, ranging from mini-rugby for young boys and girls to a veterans XV. In recent years this trend has been repeated all over Great Britain and I make special mention of the north-east only as an example and because it has always been a hotbed of soccer. Ask yourself, where were West Hartlepool as a rugby force ten years ago?

The introduction of leagues was the turning point. With titles and cups at stake, matches became more competitive and players became more professional – in attitiude if not in pocket. Businesses were quick to seize on rugby as the ideal way of reaching a market which had disposable income. Witness the tie-up of the Royal Bank of Scotland, Bell's Whisky and the top clothing manufacturer Toggi with the Scottish RU.

At Bath, as well as being involved on the coaching side, I am also the club's commercial manager, though my official title is chairman of fund-raising. When the club opened their superb new stand in 1994 we completed a deal with Teacher's Whisky worth £1 million over four years. The Teacher's Stand is a benchmark to which other ambitious clubs aspire. With its luxury executive boxes, which serve top-class cuisine to corporate diners, and its superb seating and first-class bar and catering facilities for supporters, the Teacher's Stand points the way forward for club rugby in this country.

Another reason why our game has changed, particularly on the field, was the realisation around 1986–7 that England had fallen behind countries such as New Zealand and Australia when it came to technique and fitness.

Former England coach Roger Uttley was a great player,

let us not quibble about that; not only a great player but a superb captain of both Newcastle Gosforth and England. But his achievements and skills as a player were not matched by his ability as a coach. When it came to coaching at international level, he never told us as England players how we could go out and beat the All Blacks or Aussies; never told individuals what they had to do in certain positions or situations. His motivation was good but he lacked the technical expertise required to be successful at that level. It was only when Roger stepped aside and Geoff Cooke took over in 1986 that the renaissance and upturn in fortunes for England really began.

Geoff was already aware that the England players were second-best to the New Zealand All Blacks and Australians when it came to technique and fitness. He introduced peak tests and body-fat tests for every England player and, although he encouraged us to train and bond together as a team, each one of us was also given a personal training programme suited to our individual needs. Geoff realised that it was no good giving me the same training as, say, Jonathan Webb or even Wade Dooley, because we each had different roles to play on the field and those roles demanded different types of training to enable us to perform to the best of our ability.

Training was taken very seriously. Those who didn't put in the effort found they were no longer England players. It was as simple as that. The days when a player was awarded an England cap because he was a sterling servant to his club and a jolly good chap to boot were gone.

This is not to say there wasn't a fun element to training, though. I had an old yellow T-shirt in my kit bag. At the end of each England training session my Bath team-mate Nigel Redman and I used to award it to the player we felt had coped least well in that day's training – a sort of Tour de France jersey in reverse. When the party broke up and the players returned to their respective clubs, Nigel and I would make a special award to the player who, in our considered opinion, was the overall winner of the yellow T-shirt. It was something different every time and always off the wall and wacky.

In 1988, for instance, after we lost narrowly, by 10–9, to France in Paris we gave Wakefield's Mike Harrison our Jewish chess set, comprising a king, queen, two castles, two rooks, two rabbis and eight pawnbrokers.

There was a time, in the sixties, when the selected England team would not meet up until the Friday evening before a Five Nations match. As the players were all from different clubs, how on earth could anyone possibly hope they would gel together as a team? In the seventies, though, England had a more 'professional' approach to the task in hand: the players met on a Friday morning and had a training session together on the Friday afternoon!

The Durham player of the sixties Mike Weston once told me that he was with his family on seaside holiday in Cornwall in 1966 when a guy who had been studying his face from a little way up the beach approached him. 'Excuse me, but don't I know you?' asked the man.

'Well, sort of,' said Mike, recognising Harlequins' John Spencer. 'We were in the England squad together in February for the game against Wales.'

Nowadays the set-up is totally different. The England players get together for two or three weekends before a major international, then report on the Wednesday morning prior to the game itself.

The Wednesday will begin with light training before some serious work on scrummaging. Thursdays usually involve line-outs, rucking and the formation of the team plan. The evenings are spent on tactics, with the forwards and backs getting together in their respective groups. Some more light work is done on the Friday morning, but really this session is all showmanship, with the players putting on a display for the

press and television people. It's more for the benefit of the Bill
McLarens of this world than serious training.

In 1988, before we beat Ireland 35–3 at Twickenham, we
finished the training session with a visit to the local swimming
baths. The commentator Nigel Starmer-Smith came along for
the ride and told us how he had learned to swim at his prep
school. 'When and where did you learn to swim, Gareth?' he
asked me.

'As a very small boy in the local canal,' I said, tongue
in cheek.

'In your local canal? Wasn't that difficult?'

'Not after I managed to get out of the sack,' I said.

Nigel raised his eyebrows, but his reaction made it clear
that he didn't get the gag or understand where I was
coming from at all, much to the amusement of the rest of
the England players.

On the Friday night a trip to a local cinema or theatre is
organised, or else it is everybody around the TV in the hotel
lounge to watch a video. On one such evening we went to the
theatre to see Pia Zadora in *The Diaries of Anne Frank*, the story
of the young Jewish girl who was hidden from the Nazis in the
home of a Dutch family in the Second World War.

When we returned to our hotel Geoff Cooke said he had
read in the press that Pia Zadora was terrible in the role and
wanted to know if she was really that bad.

'Put it this way, Geoff,' I said, 'when it came to the scene
where the Gestapo search the house, Dean Richards and Nigel
Redman were shouting, "She's in the attic!"'

Many players opt for a sleeping pill when they go to bed
on the Friday night. From the moment you are selected
to play for your country there is a build-up of tension,
and the night before a Five Nations game is particularly
unnerving.

On match day the players assemble for breakfast and scan

the morning newspapers. It is here that there is much ribbing before the serious part of the day unfolds.

'It says here in the *Telegraph* that you "ran to good purpose" against Scotland,' I once called out to Jonathan Webb.

'That means you were crap!' Wade Dooley interpreted.

Nowdays you're more likely to find Will Carling or Rory Underwood on portable phones to their agents, discussing endorsement deals or TV commercials. There's nothing wrong in that in my book, I just wish the authorities would drop this façade of pretending that rugby is an amateur game played by amateurs. It hasn't been that way for years.

Newspapers read, it's all aboard the team coach for an escorted drive to the ground before battle commences.

One of the secrets of England's success in the nineties has been the stability of the side. The wholesale chopping and changing of teams is a thing of the past. Players have to earn their places on merit rather than get there because they went to the 'right' university or know the 'right' people, as was sometimes the case in the past. Squad members who are getting on in years are gradually replaced, one by one, so as not to disrupt the balance of the team.

On this subject I once commented to Jack Rowell that the trick must be in pin-pointing the match when a player hasn't got what it takes at international level any more.

'The trick is in knowing in the game immediately before the game when he shows he hasn't got it any more,' replied Jack.

From 1986 onwards the England management and selectors started to get it right. To play well together you must know your team-mates well; know their strengths, weaknesses and idiosyncrasies. The selectors now seem to appreciate that, and in the nineties they have picked some very strong sides.

Unfortunately, like most British sports governing bodies, the RFU is run by committees. In the south-west we say that the good Lord created everything on earth bar the camel, which was put together by committee. If this suggests to you that I have little time for such bodies, you're dead right. I have walked through many parks in towns and cities throughout the world, but I have yet to see a statue to a committee.

It is not because of, but in spite of, fossilised committees that rugby has been dragged into the twentieth century these past few years. Geoff Cooke; Jack Rowell; South Africa's Kitch Christie; Gareth Davies, the Cardiff chief executive; Aussie coach Bob Dwyer and David Campese, amongst others, are individuals who make things happen in the game. They are people of vision who are not afraid to make daring decisions and stand up for what they believe. It is no coincidence that they are, if anything, not committee people.

During the 1991 World Cup in Great Britain and France the representatives from the five unions argued over the most trivial of things, like who was allowed to wear World Cup blazers and who wasn't; who qualified to wear the official World Cup tie; who could go to which dinners and who could sit nearest to the Queen. It was all very petty and a waste of valuable time. Sure, money was made, but not nearly the amount that should have been generated by the world's premier rugby tournament. When the 1991 World Cup financial report was finally issued, the supremo of South African rugby, Louis Luyt, said that if it had been up to him he would have 'fired the lot of them'. I tend to agree.

Cotton Traders, the company owned by former England players Fran Cotton and Steve Smith, have made rugby shirts prime leisure wear, in many cases designer wear. The English RFU committee entered into a five-year contract with Cotton Traders to produce and market the England strip back in 1991. However, many of the RFU officials were unhappy because they wanted a new strip only for the 1991 World Cup. Many of them didn't realise that the contract was binding for longer and were displeased in subsequent years because England were wearing a shirt they did not like. Don't grouse, gentlemen. It was after all, agreed by the committee!

Now that I have finished playing, the best way I can repay the sport that has given me so much is to find some way of slimming down those damn committees. I'd stop short of shooting them, of course, but not too far short.

As we move towards the year 2000 I can foresee even more changes which will alter the entire nature of the game. No one, but no one, will stop the bandwagon rolling towards professionalism or, more accurately, semi-professionalism. The move in this direction is being instigated in the main by the players. All I can say to those who believe rugby is still purely amateur and a fountain of the Corinthian spirit is, are you in touch with a planet called Earth?

In the summer of 1994 Bath were interested in the Irish international forward Nick Popplewell, who was playing his rugby in Ireland with Greystones. Nick wanted us to look into the possibility of a house, a job and a car if he were to sign for us. Fair enough, but the stumbling block was that he also wanted a guaranteed first-team place. No one at Bath will ever have that – we even have England internationals in our second XV. In the end Nick signed for Wasps. I don't know what the deal was but nowadays it would be ludicrous to think that a top international player like Nick would sign without there being some sort of deal.

Bath's Victor Ubogu made his debut for England in 1992 against Canada and was by 1994 very much a regular in the England set-up. Steve Ojomoh, on the other hand, was a newcomer to the national side, having won his first cap against Ireland earlier in the year. During the 1994–5 pre-season training Victor was sitting in the dressing room with the other players when I wandered in. Steve had picked up a nasty injury to his eye in training and I had referred him to hospital.

As I sat with my charges drinking tea after training, our team secretary, John Allen, popped his head round the door. 'Heard the news? Steve Ojomoh's got a detached retina.'

A few minutes later Victor sidled up to me. 'Is that correct about Steve having a detached retina?' he asked.

'Apparently,' I said.

'I'm not happy about that,' said Victor. 'I've been here much longer than him and I'm still living in a club flat.'

It's the way the game is going.

11

England Debut

MAKING YOUR first appearance for your country is a nerve-racking affair. You obviously want to do well and you take to the field hoping it will not be a one-off, rather the start of an illustrious international career.

I made my England debut at Twickenham in a 19–3 defeat against the touring Australians in 1984. You are usually informed of your selection by telephone. Even in 1984 the management did not tell players that they had been selected to play for England. We were simply asked whether we were 'available to play'. I don't know of anyone who has said no.

Once you inform the England management of your availability, the secretary of the RFU sends you a pack containing the match arrangements. It details what time you have to report to the hotel, when the training sessions are to take place, what you must bring in the way of kit and formal wear. If you are a new boy and don't have the official England blazer, tie and slacks, you're fitted out with them before the game.

One of the perks of playing for England is that you don't have to pay for drinks. In the past this involved players drinking in the bar reserved for them in the chosen hotel. Note the 'reserved for players'. The RFU officials and their guests had a separate bar reserved for them. They may have picked the players for the squad, but there was no way they felt they had to demean themselves by drinking with us. I'm glad to say this is no longer the case.

My first cap for England ought to have been the red-letter day of my rugby career. From the moment I learned I was in the England team I was on tenterhooks. For almost a fortnight I walked around in a dream. As for the game itself, for me it was a nightmare. Most players recall their England debuts with relish. The rugby that day against Australia and the subsequent social get-together were such an unmitigated disaster that I've tried to push them to the back of my mind ever since.

I had played for the South-West Counties against the touring Aussies. The game ended in a 12–12 draw but, if we had had a little bit more of the run of the ball, I think we might have sneaked a win. The Australians were a very hard side but played wonderful rugby with it. That particular team became the very first Aussie touring side to achieve a Grand Slam of beating all four British home nations. In Michael Lynagh at fly-half, Nick Farr-Jones at scrum-half, Andy McIntyre at prop and, of course, the great David Campese, who played on the wing on that tour, they had young players who were already top-class internationals. If that wasn't enough, in Roger Gould at full-back, Andy Slack at centre, Steve Poidevin at flanker and Steve Cutler at lock they had experience aplenty. So players have had easier England debuts.

Campese excepted, the Australians drew their strength from the suburbs around Sydney and Brisbane and so there was a very close family feel to their team. They stuck it out for one another when the going got tough and they had a good understanding of each other on the pitch. It resulted in a very fast and open game of rugby, fluid and very together. By contrast, the England team of the day were an oddball assortment with no discernible unity or sense of team spirit. In my Bath team-mates Jon Hall, Nigel Redman and Stuart Barnes,

Leicester's Rory Underwood, Chris Butcher from Harlequins and, of course, me, the England team that day had players with little or no international experience.

We needed guidance; we needed to be told what to do out on the pitch; to be coached in how to stop, then defeat, the Australians. We wanted leadership and encouragement. Instead we had a coach who seemed to want Australia to win! If anyone ever introduces an event for all-time bad coaches, Dick Greenwood would be an Olympic gold-medallist. He was the England coach of the day and was to tactics what Julian Clary is to scrummaging. To be fair, he was a fitness man, but our only hope of making a show against such a strong and technically accomplished side was to play a good tactical game.

In the few days the players got together before the game all we did was run, run and run. It was varied, mind you: sometimes we'd do shuttle runs, other times short sprints. Just so it didn't get too boring, there'd be laps of the field at three-quarter pace and, of course, all this was preceded every session by a long warm-up run.

There might have been a game plan but we players didn't get to hear of it. We didn't know one another's style of play, either, because we never had the opportunity to familiarise ourselves with each other in game situations. Having come down from Bath, where I was used to Jack Rowell's methodical and thorough approach to tactical training and coaching, it was like stepping back twenty years.

On the day of the game the England team were taken on a long walk along the banks of the river. We had assembled on the Wednesday but it wasn't until 11.45 on the Saturday morning, as we overlooked Father Thames, that we received our first and only team talk from our leader.

Dick Greenwood gathered the players around him at the riverside. 'Closer,' he said. 'So you can all hear.'

Keen as mustard to learn, I shuffled my feet along with

the others as we formed a tight-knit semi-circle around Dick, who was standing on a gentle, sloping bank to give him some elevation. We stood in silence, ears cocked, as he surveyed us all. After thirty seconds or so the coach of the England team spoke.

'England expects!' he said.

He looked at his silent charges for another thirty seconds, then gave one nod of his head as if to affirm his words. There was a pregnant, embarrassed silence.

'Is that it?' Rory Underwood whispered to me eventually.

'I think so,' I answered.

And indeed it was. Dick Greenwood extended his right arm to indicate that we should step aside to make room for him and passed among us before leading the way back to the hotel.

'England expects! Expects what? What the 'king hell is that supposed to mean?' asked Stuart Barnes.

'It has historical connotations,' said Waterloo's Jim Syddall.

'I friggin' well know where it comes from,' said Stuart. 'I'm just wondering how Alf Tupper thinks it can possibly help us.'

One thing I know for sure: if Nelson could have been around to see England play that day, by half-time he would have been wearing his patch over his good eye.

The Australians, as I say, ran out winners by 19–3 and it could and would have been more but for the fact that we English lads played for our pride. Bereft of a tactical plan, ignorant of one another's individual styles and having no game system, we had no choice but to battle for our personal and England's collective honour. We ran around like headless chickens, not knowing what we were expected to do. Only grit and hard work prevented a hugely embarrassing result.

The game itself couldn't have been more of a farce if it had been created by Ben Travers or Ray Cooney. After ten minutes Gloucester's Steve Mills, who was playing hooker, unfortunately cricked his neck and had to go off. His replacement was Coventry's Steve Brain. Nothing wrong with that – one good player for another.

Steve Brain had to come down from the part of the stand where the replacements were sitting and this involved descending a flight of steps inside the grandstand itself. When he reached the door that opened out into the tunnel, he found it was locked.

He banged and banged for fully five minutes, but because of the noise of the crowd no one could hear him. Anxious and frustrated, he set off back up the stairs to where the replacements were sitting. In full kit and leaning over the balustrade he managed to attract the attention of one of the officials down below and, having asked for the door to be unlocked, he ran back down the steps.

From his side of the door Steve heard the jangle of keys and took a deep breath as he prepared himself for the battle ahead, ever mindful of the fact that England expected. A few moments passed, then more jangling of keys, before eventually he heard a key being placed in the lock.

'This is it! The big one! I'm ready! Let's go!' he thought. Jingle, jangle again. The clunk of another key in the lock. Silence. Jingle, jangle. Clunk.

'What the 'king hell are you doing out there?' shouted Steve, hyped up to hell now and frustrated at not being able to get out on to the pitch.

'Oh dear. I think we've got the wrong keys. Hang on. Don't go away, we'll be back,' said a genteel voice from the other side of the door.

Three minutes or so passed as Steve kicked his heels in the semi-darkness before he once again heard encouraging noises from the other side.

Jingle, jangle. Jingle, jangle. Then the sound of a key in the lock. Steve took a deep breath, puffed out his chest and stamped his studs on the concrete floor. He stretched his arms upwards then drew them to his side and clenched his fists ready for battle.

Jingle, jangle. Jingle, jangle, jingle. Clunk. Then the clunk of another key, and then another. Steve let out a long, low sigh of exasperation and slumped against the wall.

''King nora!' he sighed as all the surging emotion and adrenaline he had pumped up drained away.

'Won't be long now. Funny how it's always the last key one tries that is the right one,' the upper-crust voice said. 'I say, you are still there, aren't you?'

Jingle, jangle. Jingle, jangle. Clunk. Jingle, jangle, clunk.

'I think I'll try this large silver one,' Steve heard the voice say.

Jingle, jangle. A more positive clunking. The door swung open and daylight shot across Steve's angst-ridden face.

'There! Didn't take too long, did it?' said an old man resembling Godfrey from *Dad's Army*. In his hand was a bunch of keys that would not have been out of place on the hip of a Tower of London Beefeater. Thirteen minutes after Steve Mills had left the pitch, enter his replacement, Steve Brain, to the fray.

Not knowing why a replacement hadn't come on for Mills we continued to battle on as best we could. When Steve did eventually take the field both of us were in the position of throwing in the line-outs to nineteen-year-old Nigel Redman with no jumpers' signals.

Steve Brain had been a late addition to the squad and the first time he and Nigel Redman actually met each other was out there on the pitch. Unbelievably we had done no line-out practice in our build-up to the game. We were so disorganised that the Australians had a better than even chance when we were throwing in and were bloody certainties to win possession when throwing in to Steve Cutler of New South Wales, who was at

the time without doubt the number one line-out jumper in the world.

Towards the end frustration got the better of me. The Aussie scrum-half, Nick Farr-Jones – also making his debut – and I had a few run-ins. It was niggly more than anything else, but my exasperation with the England set-up and my annoyance at the lack of organisation and preparation for a game that was my international debut finally got the better of me. Nick Farr-Jones caught me high at the edge of a maul and I let go with a right-hander that boxed his left ear flat. Nick went down like a sack of hammers. Sixty thousand people at Twickenham saw it. Fifty million TV viewers saw it. The referee, however, did not.

That one punch made me as popular as Arthur Scargill in the Monday Club. I went into the international wasteland for two years, until new blood recalled me to play in the 25–20 victory over Ireland at Twickenham in 1986.

Following any international game there is always the opportunity to revel in success or drown sorrows. The post-match dinner and ball for the Australian game was held at London's Hilton Hotel. Even after the game we England players were not given the chance to get to know one another. In its infinite wisdom the RFU had invited hundreds of stuffed shirts from such places as Oxford and Cambridge universities, Eton and Harrow schools, the Civil Service, Church of England Synod and the City. One player was placed at each table of guests.

Speaker after speaker, most of them RFU sycophants, stood and let forth a constant stream of verbal diarrhoea. There was no substance at all to what was said by any of the speakers, for if there is anything at all to be learned from such functions, it is that the human brain starts to work as soon as one is born but ceases to operate immediately such speakers take to their feet.

The speeches finally over, the band of the Welsh Guards

struck up with 'In an English Country Garden', and I foxtrotted across the floor with Nigel Redman.

'This is bloody ridiculous,' I said.

'I know,' said Nigel. 'Neither of us knows how to lead.'

Later in my international career I was to learn the secret of enjoying these old-boy RFU binges but the following day, travelling back to the West Country, I thought, 'If that was international rugby, I'd sooner play for Bath.'

12

Face Don't Fit

HAVING WON my first cap in 1984, I got into hot water with the RFU for that 'physical debate' with Nick Farr-Jones. As the referee hadn't seen the incident, I was not sent off but I was probably punished more than I would have been if he had. I was left out of the England team for almost two years. If I was overlooked because there were better forwards than me, fair enough, but I have little doubt that it was personal.

Before I appeared again for England, against Ireland in 1986, I was selected for the 1985 tour to New Zealand – only for the decision to be retracted. I received a charming letter from the RFU informing me of my selection for the tour and was naturally delighted to be back in the international fold, especially for a prestigious series against the All Blacks.

However, two days after the letter arrived I had a phone call from RFU headquarters. The official on the other end of the line was embarrassed. He had clearly been given the job of doing someone else's dirty work and it was obvious he didn't relish the task. I even detected a degree of sympathy for me in the tone of his voice.

'I'm afraid you will not be going to New Zealand after all, Mr Chilcott. Be so kind as to ignore the letter, would you?'

'How come I was selected and suddenly there has been this turn-around?' I asked, not unreasonably I felt.

There was a moment's awkward silence. Then: 'As far as the selectors are concerned, you're not the type of person they wish to see in an England shirt.'

That was it. I was furious at this slight on my character. It may have been far from unblemished to start with, but the suggestion that I was not worthy of representing the country I love filled me with rage. For a split-second I was about to tell the voice on the other end of the phone to go forth and multiply, but fortunately thought better of it. It would have been playing right into their hands.

'Is that so?' I said calmly. 'Then would you be kind enough to pass on this message from me to the selectors?'

'Erm, what exactly would that be?' the voice asked nervously.

'This situation no doubt goes back to the incident with Nick Farr-Jones,' I said. 'If that is the case, then tell the selectors to remember the words of the great bard: "Condemn the fault and not the actor of it."'

Another silence.

'Do you know, Mr Chilcott,' said the voice eventually with what seemed to me like a hint of admiration, 'when you said to pass a message on to the selectors, I thought you were going to tell them to piss off and, to be honest, I wouldn't have blamed you. For you to reply in such an eloquent and apposite manner . . . well, the selectors have obviously misjudged you and I shall tell them so.'

'Thank you,' I said, and replaced the receiver.

My fiancée, Ann, who had been listening to my side of the conversation from the adjoining room, came in.

'Gareth, that was wonderful, what you said about condemning the fault, not the actor of it. What on earth made you think of that?' she asked.

'It's written there,' I said, pointing to the small loose-leaf calendar I'd received from a firm of local builders at New Year and kept by the telephone. 'It's today's quote!'

Throughout my career I've had running battles with rugby's authorities and committees, especially disciplinary committees. In Ireland they have a saying, 'Anything is possible until it goes to committee.' How right they are! No doubt I established something of an unenviable record by being sent off five times in first-class matches and by being the recipient of the RFU's longest-ever ban of twelve months. There's a fine line between hard, aggressive rugby and downright foul play, and I must admit that in my early days in the sport, I was not too sure where to draw that line. But as I got older and played to a higher standard, eventually reaching the top, I realised that the emphasis at that level is on skill, speed and strength. You learn to channel your aggression, to control it, to win battles by speed of thought. One of the reasons I got into more trouble than most is that I don't exactly look like a genteel soul and inevitably people tend to form an opinion based on your physical appearance. Unlike far too many of the so-called hard men in rugby, I never ran crying to committees or the press when I was on the receiving end of some physical argy-bargy. As Mike Fry of Bristol told me when I was a teenager, 'Live by the sword, die by the sword.' I was prepared to do that.

What amuses me is how many of the former hard men of rugby are now on disciplinary committees and throw up their hands in horror when players appear before them for perpetrating acts they were only too happy to commit themselves only a few years before. But that's rugby players for you – we all become much better players after a year or so's retirement from the game!

The politically correct brigade will be up in arms but I've always believed that a clip around the ear for someone committing a misdemeanour brings the culprit quickly back into line without doing any great psychological damage. We once had a troublesome teenager who attended the Bath junior coaching sessions we hold at our Lambridge training ground.

'How do you handle the lad when he acts up, Coochie?' our Under-21 skipper Richard Chamberlain asked.

'When he starts to behave in an unsociable and disruptive way, I always go back to my office and take down from the shelf my copy of Piaget's *Language, Mores and Psychology of the European Teenager*. 'Really?' said Richard. 'How does that help?'

'I take it out on to the pitch and whack him over the head with it. After that, no trouble.'

I've always felt that in a great many areas my face just didn't fit. I had played for England and the British Lions, was a regular in a Bath side that won eight cup finals and five Courage League One Championships, yet it wasn't until I was about to retire from the game that I received my first invitation to play for the incongruously named Barbarians.

The Barbarians, or Baa-Baas for short, are a side selected from all clubs, both at home and abroad, whose aim it is to play open, fluid rugby of the entertaining variety while keeping to the ethos of true sporting behaviour.

The Baa-Baas first played a major touring team in 1948 when, at short notice, a match against the Australians was arranged at Twickenham. The game was actually staged to raise money for the Australians' return journey home as they were strapped for cash. I've never been able to find out why they didn't buy return tickets!

The game, which the Baa-Baas won 9–6, was such a success that a fixture with the Barbarians quickly became the final showpiece match for every touring side. The players brought together from various clubs are encouraged to indulge in the fast, open play that has been a feature of this Corinthian side since its inception in 1890.

Another feature of the Baa-Baas is that players wear the

Barbarian shirt and shorts, but the socks of their regular club.

What many do not realise is that one of the main functions of the Baa-Baas is to raise money that will be ploughed back into rugby at grass-roots level. For example, in 1995, for every try the Baa-Baas scored in any game, their sponsors, Scottish Amicable, donated £300. Over the years the exciting play and try-scoring of the Baa-Baas have led to Scottish Amicable shelling out over £50,000, all of which has been channelled into the development of youth rugby for boys and girls of all races, creeds and denominations. This can only be a good thing.

It is considered a great honour to be selected to play for the Barbarians and it was to my chagrin that, until my final playing days, I was never invited. Again, if I had not been capable of producing the fast, open rugby the Baa-Baa committee like to see, I could have understood my omission. But I heard on the rugby grapevine that I was not 'their type of nice rugby player'. Most galling of all, when Richard Hill represented the Baa-Baas, he was told that another reason I was not included was that 'Chilcott's school tie is not one we would readily recognise'. Fortunately the old-school-tie brigade who select the Barbarians sides has changed and we now have a somewhat more enlightened approach to team composition.

That's not to say that the old-school-tie mentality does not exist in rugby nowadays. It still does in some quarters but it is not as widespread as it was.

In 1993 I was in the Leicester area on business and decided to call in to see the former Leicester, England and British Lions player Peter Wheeler, whose illustrious international career between 1975 and 1984 won him 41 caps.

Ever the gentleman host, Peter served tea in his study and we put the rugby world to rights, as players do when they get together. On bidding him farewell, I stood up and picked up the tea tray from his desk, indicating to Peter that I would take it through to the kitchen for him.

'For God's sake be careful with that tray!' he said, alarmed. 'Do you know how much it cost me?'

I was a bit taken aback. It looked like a perfectly ordinary wooden tea tray to me – no embellishments, carvings or the like. But I know nothing at all about antiques or rare artifacts.

'No,' I said, holding the tray gingerly before me. 'How much?'

Peter sat back in his leather chair. 'The best part of £20,000,' he said matter-of-factly.

The teacups started to rattle as my hands began to shake. I leaned forward slowly and gently placed the tray back on Peter's desk. '£20,000?' I said, staring, mouth open, at what, as I say, looked like an everyday wooden tray to me.

'Best part of,' Peter reiterated.

Noticing my incredulity, he started to explain. 'My eldest son,' he said. 'We sent him to a public school. He was there for four years. Cost me just under £2,000 a term. In his final term he left without an examination to his name. All he left with in the end was that tray he'd made in the woodwork class. Twenty thousand quid!'

I left Peter's house wondering just how many RFU officials and Baa-Baa selectors have wooden trays like that. I bet there are quite a few.

Five Nations Tales

'France have two chances. Slim and no chance. Slim is out of town.'

Wade Dooley, Preston Grasshoppers, England and British Lions.

'When you play us you can choose your poison. The end result will be the same. You're going to die.'

Finlay Calder, Stewart's-Melville FP, Scotland and British Lions.

13

Second Time Lucky

D ESPITE THE fact that I had not enjoyed one second of my
England debut against Australia in 1984 I was thrilled to
be called up again in 1986 to face Ireland at Twickenham.

There were two differences between the game against the
Irish and the one in which I won my first cap.

First, the England coach was now Martin Green, who
possessed tactical know-how. We went on to the field to
face Ireland as a team, with a game plan that would expose
the weaknesses of the opposition and allow us to play to
our strengths. In the end we won by 25–20, but the score
makes the game sound a lot closer than it actually was. In
truth England were on top for the entire match and never
for one moment could I see us losing. Leicester's Dean
Richards, winning his first cap, went over for two tries
and Wasps' Huw Davies corkscrewed over for another.
Rob Andrew, then at Nottingham, gave a foretaste of what
was to come from his magical boot with three conversions and a penalty. Our other score came from a penalty try.

The second difference was that Martin Green ensured that
all the players had time to get to know one another, both
personally and in terms of styles of play – although, having

said that, we had in fact all been picked for our ability to fit into the system Martin had devised.

You may think it absurd that an England team could take to the field not knowing each other, but as illustrated earlier it was quite often the case until 1986 or so. Happily nowadays there is a much more — if I can use the word — 'professional' attitude to international games, one more in keeping with the approach of the other major International Board countries. As for the fiasco of my own England debut, the more I played for my country the more I realised I was not alone in my experience.

Preston Grasshoppers' Wade Dooley won his first cap for England in a 22–15 win against Romania at Twickenham the year before me, 1985. With all due respect to the 'Hoppers', the Fulwood club are not among the big boys of English club rugby and, when Wade turned up to join the squad for the Romania game, few England players knew who he was.

To give some credit to Dick Greenwood, it was he who noticed Wade's potential. I have always believed that better than ability is the ability to spot ability, and when others were looking to more fashionable clubs, Dick took in a couple of Preston Grasshoppers games. He saw what no other selector did and decided that Wade had what it took to play at the very highest level. He was proved right on this one. Wade's England and British Lions career lasted for nine years, during which he won fifty-five caps for his country.

When Wade had the telephone call from Dick saying he had been included in the England squad, he was totally overawed. 'Will any of the England team have heard of me?' he asked modestly.

'Heard of you, Wade?' said Dick encouragingly. 'Why, after the last international you were the sole topic of their conversation.'

'Me?' asked Wade incredulously.

'Yes, you! They were all saying they couldn't understand how you had never been selected for England. You're the talk of the clubs in the south.'

Buoyed up by this complete fabrication, Wade joined the England squad with more than a degree of confidence in his own ability to perform at the highest level.

England's captain against Romania was Leicester's Paul Dodge. As he came to the conclusion of his team talk before England took the field, Paul felt he had to make some mention of the debutant from the north-west.

'. . . and finally, I want you all, especially those of us with experience of games like this, to help our young debutant today,' he said. He paused for a moment as he scanned his brain for the name of the lock from Preston who was seated in front of him.

'This lad here . . . well, he wouldn't be here if he wasn't good enough. But . . .' Paul started to tail off as the name just would not come. '. . . our debutant here will not let us down, that I know. But he needs our help out there.'

Paul's face was now scarlet and his mouth dry. 'So let's get right behind . . . right behind . . .' The rest of the England team glanced alternately at Paul and Wade. An embarrassed silence descended on the dressing room.

'Right behind . . . er . . .'

Suddenly Paul's face brightened and he let out a long sigh of relief as the name came to him.

'Let's get right behind Wayne Gooley here!'

Following the victory over Ireland I started to learn how to enjoy the post-match stuffed-shirt functions. Whilst RFU officialdom and their guests were trotting their foxes, I joined a group of England players on the Hilton's roof-garden bar on the twenty-ninth floor, which affords a quite startling view of London. I was told by our captain, Wakefield's Mike Harrison, that the object of the evening from that point on was to get as many drinks on to someone else's room tab as was humanly possible. Mike, Peter Winterbottom, Stuart Barnes, Dean Richards, Wade Dooley and I gave it our best shot and, looking back, we didn't make a bad fist of it at all. Wasps' Nigel Melville ended up with just over £2,000-worth of drinks on his bill.

The RFU traditionally pay for players' drinks but there was an inquiry on the Sunday as to how Nigel had managed to run up a tab of two grand. In his defence he pointed out that there were six rooms with no drinks on their bills at all. 'As far as I am aware, there are not six teetotallers in this England team!' he told the inquiry board.

From drinking beer the six of us had graduated to cocktails at £4.50 a shot – and this was 1986, remember. Come three in the morning Dean Richards took to his feet to visit the loo and keeled over flat on his face.

'You've got to give it to Deano,' I said. 'He always knows when to quit!'

14

Pardon My French

THE FRENCH say their particular style of rugby has one quality that no other Five Nations team possesses. The quality of joy. The French play their rugby with great passion, what the Welsh call *hwyl*. But it is a passion steeped in deep seriousness. Add to this a fiery temperament, which one finds especially in the south of France, and it is hardly surprising that the pot is liable to overheat on the odd occasion.

The French style of play has great flair but they also have immense physical power to go with it. They play with a swagger and arrogance and insist on playing 'their way', even if it is getting them bloody nowhere.

Talent abounds in France but, because the game in the home countries is physical, the French sometimes feel they have to be intimidatory in order to combat this. They end up going over the top, ignoring the super rugby of which they are capable and, as we have witnessed on more than one occasion, resorting to what can only be described as thuggery, which really is beneath them.

Alain Carminati was suspended for seven months after being sent off by English referee Fred Howard in their game against Scotland at Murrayfield in 1990. There was also that notorious game at the Parc des Princes in 1992, when both Gilbert Lascubé of Agen and Victor Moscato of Bègles were dismissed for violent conduct during England's 31–13 victory. A mark of what the French selectors thought of their behaviour is that Lascubé and Moscato were not picked again for their country.

Rugby is a highly competitive sport, but French rugby is overtly so. It may have something to do with the fact that, whereas league and cup competitions are comparatively new to British rugby, the French club championship began way back in 1892. One would think that after all that time it would be well organised and work like clockwork, but the truth is that it's a complicated affair not helped by the system changing virtually every year.

The French club championship basically starts with teams playing in leagues at the start of the season. The qualifiers then move on to a knock-out stage. The eight remaining teams in the knock-out then go into a sort of premier league, with the top two competing in the actual champions' cup final. Well, that's how it worked at the time of writing but, as I say, it changes with bewildering regularity.

On my last visit to France I bumped into the great full-back Serge Blanco, capped ninety-three times, whose record thirty-eight tries for France between 1980 and 1991 I don't think will ever be beaten. I asked Serge what the system for the club championship was in that particular year.

'Furk nose, Gareth, my friend,' he said, shrugging his shoulders.

I had some battles royal with the French. I played against the gargantuan prop from Lourdes, Jean-Paul Garuet, on three occasions, in 1986, 1987 and 1989. Garuet is a hard, no-nonsense Basque, built like a beer barrel, who hates the Spanish. He even hates the French, so you can imagine what he thinks of the English.

When France triumphed 19–15 at Twickenham in 1987,

Garuet hit me with a searing haymaker between the eyes just as I was struggling to my feet from a scrum.

'Fight him back!' screamed Wade Dooley, who had witnessed the incident.

'It's hard to fight back when you're crying!' I shouted.

If I were to be asked which international rugby ground has the most atmosphere and is the most intimidating for any opposition, without doubt it would be the Parc des Princes in Paris.

The moment the England team coach arrives you are in no doubt that this stadium is the most awesome in the world. Two gigantic bronze-fronted doors that would be more at home on Ben Hur's temple creak open to allow the coach to enter. It takes three men on each gate to push them to one side. It seems to take an eternity and, while the coach idles, the Gallic faces peer up at the windows. Some just stare at you as if you have arrived from another planet. Some gesticulate wildly with their fists and shout. My French is not that good, so when they shouted at me I didn't know what they were actually saying. From their facial expressions and gritted teeth, however, I knew it wasn't 'Hiya, Gareth, how's the wife and kid?'

Your stomach starts to churn as your nervous system begins to do the rumba. It is here, in a foreign country, in the heart of opposition territory, that you must have the utmost self-confidence. If you are not careful, your nerves can get the better of you and self-doubt starts to creep in. If a player lets that happen he starts to think, 'Why am I here? Why me? Surely there are better forwards than me? Why didn't so-and-so from Wasps get picked? He was great against us in that club match.' You have to tell yourself you are the best. That there is no one better in that particular position. That the management and selectors are brilliant because they got it dead right.

After what seems an age the massive gates to the Parc des Princes finally open wide to allow the coach to enter the

stadium and those random thoughts disappear as your mind turns to the abyss that opens up before you. For abyss it is. As the coach enters it descends and descends into the black bowels of this fearsome stadium.

The coach halts in what seems like an underground car park, except that there are no other vehicles to be seen. It is dark and eerie and even the softest speech echoes and rebounds off the cold concrete walls.

Down in the changing room you are left to your own devices and desires. You are far removed from the atmosphere of a top international game. You cannot hear the crowd in the stadium and you are not aware of the hordes thronging on the pavements outside. If it wasn't for the chatter of your fellow England players, there would be total silence.

When the buzzer sounds to signal that the teams should take to the pitch, you embark on the longest walk in rugby. Flight after flight of concrete steps have to be gingerly negotiated on aluminium studs. As Wade Dooley once said as we made the ascent, 'Bugger the game. I'm always knackered by the time I reach the top of these stairs.'

From the darkness of the coach concourse in the depths of the stadium, up through the artificial light of the corridors and concrete steps, your eyes adjust to the half-light. As you ascend the very last step and raise your body to ground level two things hit your senses with sledgehammer ferocity. A blinding, intense light and the ear-splitting roar of the 80,000-strong crowd.

Your eyes accommodate the light very quickly but your ears never adjust to the resounding noise. The roof of the stadium not only encircles the stands but overlaps the pitch and overhangs in a downward curve, so the clamour of the crowd doesn't evaporate on the wind but stays within the stadium. The sound is deflected back down on to the pitch and when the spectators are vociferous it is literally impossible to hear a team-mate who is shouting to you from only two yards away.

That is why teams who play France at this super stadium hardly ever communicate with one another verbally. All the England line-out calls and the captain's instructions for back-row moves are signalled by hand. If you are ever lucky enough to go to the Parc des Princes, or if you are watching on the TV a Five Nations game from Paris, look out for the hand signals. This mode of communication between players happens at no other ground. If you have ever been to a rock concert and experienced 'buzz lugs' after the show from the amplified sound, you will know exactly how your ears feel in the dressing room after a game at the Parc des Princes.

The scrum-half forms the vital link between the pack and the backs. He is the player most likely to get tackled, so in order to play well in that role in top-class rugby you must be swift-footed as well as quick-witted. If you are very fast over ten yards like Richard Hill was, then you become the player most likely to get late-tackled. This is exactly what happened to Richard fifteen minutes into the second half of England's game against France in Paris in 1986, a match in which France had the upper hand, going on to win 29–10. Opposing scrum-half Pierre Berbizier, who played for Lourdes and Agen, was a world-class player. Like those of Serge Blanco, Jean-Pierre Rives and Jean-Paul Garuet, Berbizier's international record is mighty impressive. He played fifty-six times for France between 1981 and 1991 and was highly respected by his opponents, who were nonetheless aware that he could on occasions be a nasty piece of work on the pitch.

My Bath colleague Richard Hill joined the match after twenty-four minutes, replacing the injured Nigel Melville. In the second half Pierre Berbizier caught Richard with a tackle that was so late I'm sure he actually launched it in the first half! That said, it was one of Berbizier's more humane tackles in that he took Richard out around about the neck.

Richard may not have been the biggest or hardest man in

international rugby but he took no nonsense from anybody, no matter what his reputation. Having witnessed the incident I knew it would be only a matter of time before Richard would be giving Berbizier some of his own medicine.

In a game there are two battles: one between the teams, the other an individual battle with your opposite number. Win your personal battles and your side will be well on its way to victory. In junior club rugby I have often seen players squaring up to one another as their 'personal battle' overheats. The referee intervenes and, more than likely, the player who is retaliating to a foul finds himself in hot water and perhaps sent off. In top-class rugby the trick is not to react straight away but to bide your time, as Richard did this day.

If a player late-tackled or subjected me to some other form of foul play liable to hurt me, I'd let it ride for a while. To show him I was not to be messed with, I'd wait ten minutes or so, then at the next available opportunity, really let him know I was still on the pitch. That way the referee would never connect the two incidents. He'd treat them as isolated occurrences and not see me as escalating trouble. A word in my ear as he ran by would be sufficient admonishment.

Richard Hill did likewise. He waited ten minutes before literally seizing his opportunity in a maul.

For those not familiar with the term, a maul is like a ruck in rugby in that it's an informal, impromptu social get-together between the forwards and a few close friends. Berbizier was in a maul situation when Richard thrust his hand amongst the two writhing and heaving sets of players. Now, you only have to shake hands with Richard to know that he has a very firm grip — and that is when he is being sociable and nice!

To have his hand gripping your balls when he is angry must be excruciating, but that's what Richard did then. When you do that to someone there are two options open to you. You can give them a good squeeze and then get out of the way as fast as you can, or you can give them a good squeeze plus a twist for good measure and then make an exit like a rat out of a viaduct, which is what Richard did.

As he sprinted away to keep up with play as the ball broke, he was surprised, to say the least, to see Berbizier doing likewise, apparently none the worse for his ordeal.

Looking back over his shoulder to where the maul had taken place, Richard experienced 'the prickling forehead' from the adrenaline racing around his head with the fear of the sight which greeted him. There on the ground was the giant French prop Jean-Paul Garuet, writhing in agony and clutching his groin.

No one likes to lose, but when you do, you must take defeat on the chin and not sulk about it. You may have seen the opposition as bitter rivals during the course of a game, but once the final whistle is blown it is all over. Most players, myself and Richard Hill included, never took the intense rivalry and physical contest into the dressing room or to the post-match dinner.

On the evening after the French game, having attended the official dinner, pockets of players from both sides sat around the hotel dining room drinking and discussing the match, rugby in general and swapping gossip. Richard spotted Jean-Paul Garuet sitting on his own at one of the long dining tables and decided to have a chat with the great man.

They talked about that afternoon's game and were quite sociable and friendly until the midway stage of the second half popped up in conversation.

'I was een a maul,' said Garuet, staring off into the distance, eyes glazed, the anger welling up inside him as he recalled the incident. 'And one of your team, the dairty cowardly sheet-house, grabbed my boll-ocks.'

Richard took a large swig of his lager.

'Eef I find out who deed that, I weel break his scrawn-nee furking neck!' Garuet went on, snarling and clenching and twisting his right hand.

Richard took another swig, stood up and wiped his mouth with the back of his hand. 'That Gareth Chilcott is a dirty little bastard! We all tell him he shouldn't do things like that,' he said, before making his excuses to leave.

As the saying goes, with friends like Richard, who needs enemies?

15

Oh Boyo

IN 1987 England were poised to win the Five Nations Championship. All we had to do was beat Wales at Cardiff Arms Park. The fact that England had not beaten Wales there since their 13–6 victory there in 1963 in the days of Richard Sharp and John Owen mattered little to us: the Welsh were going to get done and that was that.

Once the England team coach crosses the Severn and reaches Chepstow, it starts: the snarling, the two-fingered gestures, the fist-waving, the tirade of obscenities and insults, the spitting at the coach windows – and that's just the girls! Hostile is too mild a word for the reception the England team receives. Players like Orrell's England scrum-half, Dewi Morris, who was born in Wales of Welsh parents but qualified to play for England, are subjected to even worse. Strange, then, that Dewi's opposite number in the Welsh side of the nineties, Llanelli's Rupert Moon, who was born in Walsall of English parents, never had to run a gauntlet of foul-mouthed abuse from English fans. But that's the Welsh – they love their country and they love their rugby, and I wouldn't want them to be any other way. Go there on anything but rugby business and they are among the best hosts you could ever wish to meet.

I can remember the weather on 7 March 1987. The sky was

the colour of a non-stick frying pan and the rain drizzled down constantly.

Our captain, Richard Hill, assembled us all in the spacious L-shaped lounge of our hotel for his captain's talk before the coach took us to the Arms Park. At first he was calm. He reminded us how we had beaten Wales 21–18 the previous year and one by one he went through the characteristics as he saw them of the Welsh players.

'Ieuan Evans. Winning only his second cap. Second cap! He'll never win another. Hasn't got what it takes. John Devereux – about as useful as a chocolate fireguard! Phil Davies – can't bloody well walk, never mind run! Paul Moriarty. Like the Moriarty in the Sherlock Holmes story, he's heading for his big fall! Mike Griffiths. If he had half a brain he'd be dangerous. I've looked up "quality forward" in the dictionary and it said, "Not Mike Griffiths"!'

And so Richard went on, running down each of the Welsh players. That done, he started to wind us all up. He began like a steam train begins a journey, slowly at first; then, when he had a full head of steam, he gained momentum until eventually he blew his top. Every other word was effing this and effing that. Sometimes he couldn't even manage a whole word without an 'effing' in the middle of it, like 'com-effing-petitive'. It was totally out of character, but the more Richard launched himself into his talk the more heated and foul-mouthed he became.

There was a moment when I thought I saw the haemorrhage moving up the side of his face. He just became more and more animated, like an X-rated Basil Fawlty.

Eventually, Richard noticed Wade Dooley, Rory Underwood, Graham Dawe, Peter Winterbottom and me cringing. 'Yes, yes!' he screamed. 'I see you effing cringing because you effing well, effing know we're going to effing well knock their effing Welsh brains in!'

Wade and I both slowly shook our heads from one side to the other.

'But we will, boys! We effing well will!' Richard shrieked, his voice now shrill and a manic smile on his face.

I raised the first finger of my right hand and pointed over his shoulder to what I and the rest of the boys could see. Which was a group of English RFU officials and their wives, led by RFU technical director Don Rutherford, along with the Protestant and Catholic bishops of Cardiff.

'No you effing well can't go to the effing toilet now!' screamed Richard. 'Put your effing hand down, Coochie.'

I lowered my finger, but immediately raised it again.

'Effing Welsh bastards! Effing Welsh bastards! We're going to effing do them for effing sure!' Richard roared at the top of his voice. Wide staring eyes raised to the ceiling, he stood wringing his wrists, the madness almost complete.

'Skipper?' I said softly, before repeating myself in a slightly louder voice. 'Skipper?'

'What? Effing what?' Richard said in a piercing voice as he came out of the trance into which he had induced himself. 'What do you effing well want? Do you want to effing well do effing Welshmen like I effing well do or not?'

Slowly, silently and very calmly, Wade Dooley joined me in pointing towards the white-faced, open-mouthed party that stood, disgusted, mortified, shocked and horrified, with raincoats draped over arms, staring at the back of the head of the captain of the England team.

At last Richard realised that something was very wrong. He froze. His shoulders suddenly hunched as if he were preparing to face the devil himself. Slowly he turned until he saw the stony, staring faces of the officials and religious leaders.

For a second or two you could have heard a pin drop. I thought Richard was gathering his thoughts to offer the most profuse apology that had ever been made in the history of mankind. How wrong I was. Slowly his right hand began to rise from his side. It gained momentum. The index finger pointed forward as he stared at the Catholic bishop, dressed in a bright red clerical tunic under a worsted jacket.

'Bastard!' screamed Richard at the top of his voice. 'That bastard is wearing one of their jerseys!'

Wade and I leaped forward, propelled Richard on to a nearby sofa and smothered his head with cushions as the outraged party, their heads thrown back and noses pointing to the ceiling indignantly, marched out.

There are times when a team can be too hyped up. The minds of the players are filled with too much emotion and not enough reason. The England forwards went out that day obsessed with battering Welshmen and we blew it.

All credit to the Welsh lads in that match. They fought with us tooth and nail but also managed to play the bit of rugby that won the day. England never played their normal game, partly because we were too concerned with getting physically involved with the opposition and partly because Wales didn't allow us to play our normal game.

Wade Dooley, Graham Dawe and myself were over the top from the moment the game started, too bothered about getting the man rather than the ball. Ball? For the first ten minutes they could have taken the ball off the park and none of us would have noticed.

In the first line-out Llanelli's Phil Davies sustained a fractured cheekbone.

'We Welsh lads can take this battering all afternoon,' Bob Norster said, wiping blood from his mouth.

'Good!' snarled Big Wade. 'Because you're going to bloody well have to!'

The Oxbridge boys in the England team like Marcus Rose kept well out of it, and who can blame them?

'Come on, boys. Don't you think it's all getting a teeny

bit too agitated?' Rosey said, hands on knees, as he watched Bob Norster and me rolling on the ground administering punches to one another's faces and ribs.

Bob broke from trying to bite my ear off to address Rosey. 'Now you know what it's like to be an abattoirer!' he snarled.

'You mean an arbitrator?' said Rosey.

'Not with the amount of blood you're going to see this afternoon!'

After ten minutes of open warfare Wales decided to get on with the game and play some open rugby, whereas we continued to run around like headless chickens, wanting to kick and thump anyone in a red jersey. Graham Dawe even had his eye on the Catholic bishop of Cardiff up in the main stand.

Swansea's Robert Jones was kicking magnificently. Neath's Stuart Evans scored a fine try and Swansea's Mark Wyatt kicked four penalties. The scoreboard said 19–12 but the Welsh did us good and proper.

I was banned after that game. I wasn't proud – I have never been proud of the fact that I have been sent off five times for violent play and hold a record ban of twelve months meted out by the RFU. Ask anyone who knows me, however, and they'll tell you that those sendings-off and bans are not a true reflection of how I played the game. A fair reflection would have seen me sent off twenty times and banned for life!

16

Calcutta Cup Furore

T HE SCOTLAND versus England Five Nations game at Murrayfield in March 1990 will never be forgotten. Everyone thought that England, having beaten Wales (34–6), Ireland (23–0) and France (26–7), would steamroller Scotland to achieve a Grand Slam and the Five Nations Championship. Scotland, for their part, had also beaten Wales, Ireland and France, so this match was the showdown, with the Five Nations title, Grand Slam, Triple Crown and Calcutta Cup all at stake on this one game.

It turned out to be Scotland's day. Their captain, David Sole, a former team-mate of mine at Bath, led his battling side to a great 13–7 victory, and who can say that on the day it was not well deserved?

The game also gained notoriety and headlines in the press and on national TV and radio for what happened afterwards to the Calcutta Cup. The true story of what happened to that treasured rugby trophy has never been told – until now, that is.

The Calcutta Cup is awarded every year to the winners of the England – Scotland game. No other countries are involved. The cup itself was made from melted-down silver rupees which the members of the ex-pat Calcutta Football Club in India donated when they closed due to lack of opposition. This speaks volumes about the mentality of the people who went off building empires. They form a rugby club, in India of all places, and are then dumbfounded when they realise they haven't got anyone to play against. By the same strange logic, for eighteen months Baker Street was London's first and only underground station. Where the hell did the trains go to?

The Calcutta Cup is a tapered cup with three snake handles and an elephant for a lid. The inscription on it reads:

> THE CALCUTTA CUP
> PRESENTED TO THE RUGBY
> FOOTBALL UNION
> BY THE CALCUTTA FOOTBALL
> CLUB AS AN INTERNATIONAL
> CHALLENGE TROPHY
> TO BE PLAYED FOR ANNUALLY BY
> ENGLAND AND SCOTLAND
> 1878

Although England and Scotland have been playing one another on an annual basis since 1871, the cup was not introduced, as the inscription testifies, until 1878. In those formative days of organised rugby the game was a lot different from that of today.

The scoring system was different for a start, and didn't reward players for scoring tries. Points-scoring was not introduced at all until 1886, when Scotland, Ireland and Wales formed an International Board. Even then the respective countries operated different scoring systems. So those early encounters in rugby's oldest international fixture, between England and Scotland, produced some strange results.

At The Oval in 1874 the English press were full of praise for England's win. Yet there were only two scores in the match — England dropped a goal while the Scots had the only try. By today's values Scotland would have won the game 5–3.

A uniform points system – one point for a try, two for the conversion, two for a penalty goal, three for a dropped goal and three for the now obsolete goal from mark – was finally introduced in 1890, when England joined the International Board. But until then the home nations haggled and argued endlessly and could not agree on which system to adopt. Some things never change!

To players and fans on both sides of the border the Calcutta Cup fixture is steeped in history and has always been special. The 1938 meeting between the two sides, for example, was the first rugby international in the world to be televised – by the BBC, of course. Throughout history the rivalry between the two nations has been intense and this instilled itself in the rugby clashes between them right from the word go.

The 1884 international was played at the Rectory Field, Blackheath. Towards the end referee George Scriven, who had played international rugby for Ireland the previous season, allowed an England score which came from a 'knock-back' by one of the Scottish players. A volatile argument ensued between Mr Scriven and both sets of players, with the Scots convinced they'd been 'done'. The argument lasted for a full ten minutes before officials restored order. The try stood and England converted it to clinch the game. During the post-match reception for the players the Scots not only refused to speak to the English team but stood with their backs to them for the best part of the night until Tom Ainslie of Edinburgh Institute Former Pupils announced that he had lost his wallet containing the then princely sum of £5.

'I'll pay two shillings to anyone who finds it and returns it to me. It has £5 in it,' Ainslie shouted to the assembled players and officials.

'In that case I'll offer five shillings!' shouted William Bolton, the England and Harlequins player.

Cue fisticuffs.

If England thought the matter would end there, they had another think coming. So outraged were the Scots that they refused to turn up for the following year's fixture at Raeburn Place in Edinburgh. What's more, a couple of Scottish officials were solicitors and they decided to take the RFU to court over the incident of the 'knock-back try' in an attempt to get the referee's decision reversed or the result quashed.

On-the-field hostilities between the two nations resumed in 1887 but the incident of the knock-back try wouldn't go away. The process of law being what it is, the case progressed at a snail's pace until it was eventually referred to the highest court of law in the land, the House of Lords. The Lords turned down the Scottish appeal, ruling that players and officials must accept the decisions of the appointed referee. The try and the result stood.

The Scots were furious, believing they had been 'turned over' by Sassenach law, and to be fair, they probably had a point. They refused to play England for two years. And modern-day players are accused of killing the true spirit of rugby by taking games far too seriously!

For the showdown Calcutta Cup game of 1990 a big question-mark must hang over the England captain Will Carling. I don't believe he took the right options that day. I thought that Harlequins' Brian Moore simply took on too much.

We were playing against the wind and there was conflict between Will Carling and Brian as to what the team should be doing. In the last half-hour the game drifted away from England. We could play a wet game, a dry game, a wide game or a tight game, but what we couldn't do was play two different games in the same match.

Our tactics were not working and we found it difficult to rework a game plan there and then out on the field. With fifteen minutes remaining the England team had a disorganised look about it. Trailing with ten minutes to go, they ended up running around in a blind panic.

A try from my Bath team-mate Jerry Guscott and a penalty from Nottingham's Simon Hodgkinson were not enough for England. Scotland won 13–7 and it was a well-deserved victory. England had not played well on the day but I'm a firm believer that a team plays as well as it is allowed to play. Many of the England team were confused as to what our game was supposed to be that afternoon, Will's or Brian's. Scotland didn't allow us to play either of them.

The post-match dinner for the players started to get very edgy as the night wore on. The Scottish team were in their formal dress of the kilt and as the drinks flowed you could feel the auld tension rising.

The Scottish lads were cock-a-hoop and we England players forlorn. There, in front of the English table, was a constant reminder of our own shortcomings and the consequence of our defeat. The Calcutta Cup, flanked by two security guards and bedecked in blue and white ribbons, sat on a small table staring back at us in unattainable smugness.

Jibes and insults began to be traded as more drink flowed.

'I hear you've got a book out that's a best-seller up here in Scotland,' Dean Richards said to Melrose's Craig Chalmers.

'Aye, that's true enough,' said Craig.

'What's it called, *Indoor Games for Flag Days?*' inquired Dean.

More and worse followed.

Hawick's Derek Turnbull and England's Paul Rendall were reported in the press as having had a 'set-to', but it was nothing really. I've been involved in a number of 'set-tos' in my time and this was no more than handbags at twenty paces. The real trouble was to follow.

England's Dean Richards and Scotland's John Jeffrey were about the only two players who had not been involved in any heated exchanges all evening. Instead they had simply sat and nattered away to one another while downing copious amounts of alcohol.

'Another gin and tonic? Double?' I heard Dean ask John.

'Go on, then,' John said.

'Do you want a slice of lemon in this one?'

'When I want lemonade, I'll ask for it!' said John.

As the night drew to a close, the two security men literally dropped their guard. Dean and John sidled up to the small table where the much-prized trophy was displayed in all its splendour. Neither is the fastest of men and their movements were slower due to the alcohol but, before anyone noticed, they had managed to swipe the Calcutta Cup and smuggle it out of the room.

Ten minutes later all hell broke loose when the 'eagle-eyed' guards alerted officials that the sacred Calcutta Cup had been purloined. The search was on and, when the Scottish RU officials couldn't find the cup, they flapped like chickens in the henhouse when the fox pays a visit.

The officials might not have been able to find it anywhere but I saw the Calcutta Cup three times after that.

On the first sighting it was being drunk from by the Scottish lads in the Tam o'Shanter pub. The second time it was on Derek Turnbull's head as he and a number of his Scottish team-mates made their way down Princes Street looking for a night-club.

At around a quarter to three in the morning I was leaving a night-club off St Andrew's Square and had turned into George Street to try to find a cab to take me back to the England hotel when I heard a clanking sound. Further down George Street

I saw the Calcutta Cup for the third time. Dean Richards and John Jeffrey were kicking it along the street like a tin can, shouting, 'I bet Oor Wullie nivver played footy with a tinnie like this!'

Later that day the Sunday news bulletins carried the story of how the Calcutta Cup had been accidentally dropped during the post-match dinner and had been taken to an Edinburgh silversmith's so that 'a dent may be repaired'.

Dent? According to Scott Hastings and some of the other Scottish lads who saw it, the old cup looked like an apprentice sheet-metal worker's practice plate!

The Scottish RU played down the incident and the extent of the damage to the old cup. However, I've heard the bill ran to a few thousand pounds. The Scottish RU conducted an internal inquiry and warned players of the dire consequences they would face if anything similar happened again. Dean and John had their wrists slapped and were banned for one international, but the other Scottish players involved got away with it because the Scottish RU feared that, if they took out their wrath on the players, the true extent of the damage inflicted on the cup when it was in their care would be leaked to the media.

I don't know who the silversmith who repaired the cup was but he or she did a remarkable job. I've seen it on a number of occasions since that infamous incident and it looks in pristine condition.

The footnote to this game really concerns its beginning. The England team arrived at Murrayfield for the showdown and first off the coach was my fellow forward Wade Dooley. He is normally a very mild-mannered and polite guy, until faced with officious 'jobsworths'.

A lot of development was taking place at Murrayfield, which was to result in the superb stadium there today. We had been told that the internal layout of the main stand was different.

''Scuse me, where are the new changing rooms at?' Wade asked a snooty commissionaire on the door.

The silver-haired commissionaire looked down his nose at Wade before replying, slowly and methodically, 'This is Scotland. Here we speak the Queen's English. We do not end a sentence with a preposition.'

'OK,' said Wade, throwing his kit bag over one shoulder. 'Where are the new changing rooms at, wanker?'

Designer Wear and the Diver

A T VARIOUS times during my rugby playing career I ended up in difficult situations and found myself feeling very uncomfortable. At Bisham Abbey, where the England team gathered for a few days' training before the 1987 Five Nations tournament, I shared a room with Northampton's Gary Pearce and Bath's Jon Hall.

I awoke one morning after the squad had enjoyed a social get-together the night before to find Jon's suitcase lying open on the floor. Inside were six or seven top designer casual shirts, his pride and joy. They were covered in a pile of vomit. Gary Pearce, who could get drunk on a wine gum dropped in a bucket of water, lay pole-axed next to the suitcase.

'What're you staring at, Coochie?' Jon asked, waking and raising himself up on one elbow. 'Those shirts are still in my suitcase, aren't they? I mean, no one has nicked them, have they? They cost me a fortune, you know.'

I told Jon his shirts were still in the suitcase.

'Colourful, aren't they?' he said proudly.

'You don't know the half of it,' I replied, racking my brain as to how I could break the news to him gently.

During the 1987 World Cup in Australia, captain Mike Harrison, Nigel Redman, Jon Webb, Peter Winterbottom,

Wade Dooley, Graham Dawe and I went scuba-diving off Hamilton Island, by the Great Barrier Reef.

Graham Dawe is to swimming what I am to hang-gliding, so he had to be coerced into going along with gentle lessons in a swimming pool. Out at sea, when it came to his turn to dive, he wasn't under the water long before he started to suffer from anxiety.

As the players on deck looked on, Graham surfaced and all seemed fine. We had been instructed that immediately on surfacing and touching the water-level platform, we must take off the mask; secondly, we should remove the weight belt; thirdly, take off the aqualung.

Graham removed his mask but, unbeknown to us, he forgot to take off his weight belt. Wade, Mike and company unwittingly looked on, sipping orange juice and crushed ice, as the weight around Graham's waist dragged him head-first back into the depths. As his feet disappeared from sight Nigel Redman shouted down to where Jon Webb and I were preparing bowls of nibbles in the galley.

'Graham's really getting into this diving thing,' he called enthusiastically. 'He surfaced, took off his mask, then immediately dived head-first back down to the bottom.'

Aware of Graham's anxiety and lack of confidence in the water, Jon and I immediately exchanged worried looks.

In seconds we were both climbing the ladder from the galley as fast as we could. The water was turquoise blue but fortunately clear as a bell. As we scrambled on to the deck we had a clear view of Graham, some fifteen feet down, legs and arms flailing as he struggled to bring himself back to the surface. Jon and I immediately jumped off the side and swam down to Graham, who was by now panic-stricken. As we struggled to rid him of his weight belt, we were joined underwater by Mike Harrison and Nigel and, working together, we managed to bring our team-mate to the surface. Wade and Peter were on hand to pull the gasping Graham on board and lay him out on the deck on his stomach.

Wade gently tilted Graham's head to one side as we all looked on, deeply concerned about his condition.

'Graham,' said Wade in a concerned voice. 'You were bloody close to drowning down there. I'm going to put pressure on your back to pump the water off your lungs.' He positioned Graham's arms flat on the deck above his head. 'Tell me, are you comfortable?'

Graham coughed and spluttered. 'Well, I've got a bit in the building society,' he replied in earnest, 'and Richard Hill's looking into a PEP savings plan for me.'

18

England Build-Up

1.00 p.m.
On the coach journey from the hotel to Twickenham hardly anyone speaks. Most players stare blankly out of the window. I try reading a newspaper. I reach across to where Rob Andrew is sitting and pick up the *Guardian* he has brought for the journey but hasn't opened. I start to read an article about soccer player Gary Mabbutt. I read the first paragraph three times but still none of it registers with me. I throw the *Guardian* back on to Rob's seat.

I feel I need something less demanding. I pick up the *Daily Star*, great for sport. They, too, have a piece on Gary Mabbutt. The first paragraph consists of two and a half lines. I read it three times. It still doesn't register. I join the rest of the players in staring blankly out of the window.

As we near Twickenham the motorcycle escort guides our coach through supporters who seem to be wandering aimlessly. It is as if they can't make up their minds whether to call into another pub or to get into the ground early and savour the build-up. They're in good spirits and, when they see our coach, they either cheer or catcall and boo, depending on which favours they are wearing.

A fist bangs on the window and makes me jump.

'Get your bloody hair cut, Chilcott, you bastard!' screams an opposing supporter who seems to have all the nation's bad teeth in his mouth.

A group of supporters bedecked in red, white and blue are standing on the kerbside. As our coach passes they smile and burst into spontaneous applause. I smile back and raise my right hand six inches in acknowledgement.

As we near Twickenham the throng of supporters is more dense. Fans from both sides mingle. It all seems friendly and convivial.

1.25 p.m.

Our coach lurches into the Twickenham car park. There is the creaking noise of the handbrake being put on and a hissing sound, like a hundred bicycle tyres being deflated at once, as our driver applies the airbrakes. I'm overcome with the strange feeling that there is no turning back. The coach driver appears so confident and relaxed about what he has to do. Dudley Wood, the RFU secretary, seems calm and in total control of himself as he issues instructions to us all. Why the hell am I nervous about what I have to do?

It has been a relatively short journey but most of the players stretch as they take to their feet.

We are wearing navy blazers with a red rose motif sewn on to the jacket pocket, white shirts, traditional red ties bearing the white rose motif with 'England RFU' embroidered below, and grey slacks. As I alight from the coach it occurs to me that the trousers I am wearing are a very good fit. As one who can never find trousers to fit me properly, I make a mental note to ask where the RFU found a shop with trousers to fit me off the peg.

With the exception of our boots, none of the players carry any kit or bags. Everything we need has been taken to the ground in a wicker skip an hour or so ago. As we walk the few yards from our coach to the Players' Entrance, I stop and sign autographs.

'Where'd you find that one?' I ask a man in his seventies who has produced a scrapbook containing a photograph of me when I first joined Bath as a seventeen-year-old. I have a mop of black hair and I'm staring up from the purple sugar-paper page like an overfed cherub.

The man is what we refer to as an 'anorak'. Instead of replying to my question with a simple one-line answer, he proceeds to tell me in protracted detail how he came by the old clipping. I stand and listen politely for a minute or so, wondering why the hell it is always me who picks them. I look up and see my team-mates disappearing into the Players' Entrance.

'OK, Pop, I gotta go. Enjoy the game,' I say as I hand him back his scrapbook, duly signed. It occurs to me that I didn't hear a word he said to me.

'He's fooking mad, he is,' says another odd-looking supporter, pointing to the old boy. 'He's never been to a game in his life.'

'Pop's all right!' I hear myself telling supporter number two as I enter the ground.

'He's fooking mad, he is,' he repeats, drooling saliva.

The dressing rooms at Twickenham are huge. In fact they are too big, the size of your average village hall. We players congregate together at the end nearer the door, partly to create atmosphere and partly out of the need to draw a sense of security from one another.

At the far end of the dressing room are two tables on which have been placed books, photographs and balls which people want signed. One by one we shuffle by and scribble our autographs on whatever needs signing. Wasps' Steve Bates is one of the replacements. It is his first time with England. He asks what the chances are of the opposition signing something so he can have a souvenir of the occasion. I tell him we do this after the game.

1.40 p.m.

There is a large brown teapot on a tray on the physio's bench, steaming like an old railway engine at rest in a siding. I pour some tea into one of the white plastic cups. It takes about one millionth of a second for the heat to permeate through the thin cup and burn my fingers.

I wander out of the dressing room and down the corridor to join the rest of the lads in taking a look at the pitch. I expect it to be medium to firm with plenty of grass on it. It will take a medium stud, but I'll wear long.

As I emerge from the end of the tunnel it seems very light, even though the day is grey and overcast. Knots of spectators are dotted around the ground already. They shout when they see us, voices echoing like those of impish boys indulging in horseplay in a cathedral.

'Looks OK,' I say to Paul Ackford, nodding towards the pitch.

'Yeah, suits me,' says Ackers.

'That shower of rain we had this morning has given it just that bit of give,' I remark.

Ackers tests the pitch with the heel of his right shoe. 'Yeah,' he says as he tries to wipe the soil on the heel of his shoe on to the grass.

Bill McLaren from BBC Television has grabbed Will Carling and is interviewing him at the side of the pitch. A girl of around twenty-three, carrying a clipboard and wearing headphones, a lumberjack shirt over the top of black jeans and Tracker boots looks very harassed as she runs from player to player asking each if he is Paul Ackford. She heaves a sigh of relief as she finally comes across Ackers. She is around 5ft 5, he 6ft 8, and they make a comical sight as she drags the reluctant but compliant player by the hand to where Bill McLaren is standing.

'Looks OK,' I say to Wade Dooley, referring to the pitch again.

'Yeah, looks OK,' he agrees.

'That shower this morning has given it just a bit of give.'

Wade nods. We are joined by Peter Winterbottom.

'Looks OK,' I say to Peter.

Peter grunts and nods, which is about the best you get from him.

'That shower this morning has given it just a bit of give,' I say.

Peter nods and grunts again.

There's little point in hanging about, so I decide to return to the dressing room. I walk past Paul Ackford, who is now being interviewed by Bill McLaren.

'We had a shower of rain this morning,' Ackers tells Bill, 'and it has given the pitch that little bit of give.'

1.50 p.m.

Back in the dressing room I start to hang up my clothes. Each player has his own peg on which his strip hangs. As you enter the door, the first peg on the left is for full-back Jon Webb, and so they continue clockwise according to the formation of the team. The next peg is for the right wing, the third for the centre, and so on until you reach the pegs for the replacements, which have tracksuits and sweatshirts in addition to the strip. The replacements are in a peculiar situation. If the team does well and wins, they won't have been a part of it. If England play badly and lose, then they can't be blamed as they won't have contributed to that either. Being a replacement means you are constantly at odds with your loyalties. One side of you wants the team to win – it is your team and they are your team-mates, after all. But there is another part of you that will not be overtly disappointed if they lose, because it might give you the opportunity to get a place in the next starting line-up. This is not selfishness, it is human nature. Ask any replacement in top-class rugby or any substitute in soccer and they will tell you it is true of everyone.

Each player is supposed to sit at his designated peg but some have favourite or 'lucky' pegs. Rory Underwood takes his strip to a peg on the other side of the room, next to Gary Pearce.

2.00 p.m.

I take my time getting ready and exchange idle chat with Jon Webb and Will Carling. I look up and see that Rory Underwood and Rob Andrew have changed already. Jon starts to do the crossword in *The Times*.

'Seven-Up is lemonade,' I tell him.

Wade Dooley rants to himself as he changes. Peter Winterbottom changes in silence, and as usual speaks only when he is spoken to and even then with a rare economy of words.

2.10 p.m.

The physio, Kevin Murphy, is giving rub-downs on the bench in the centre of the room. The room reeks of liniment and Deep Heat rub. The only real ventilation comes when someone opens the door. The vapour is so strong that my eyes start to water. I make my way to the shower area to rinse them with cold water. Brian Moore, 'Pit Bull' as we call him, is in the shower area. He is fully changed and rants and raves as he walks up and down the shower area. As I rinse my face in a washbasin I hear a dull thudding noise. I turn to see Brian gritting his teeth and banging his forehead against the tiled wall of the shower. I wonder what supporter number two would make of Brian if he could see him now.

Face dry, I walk past Brian, making no acknowledgement of

his presence. He's best left alone in his own world until he works himself up into the mental state he feels he needs to be in.

Every player is busying himself with his kit except for Mike Teague, who has only removed his blazer. He sits cross-legged, reading a copy of the match programme and chewing on gum, seemingly oblivious to all the activity going on around him.

Our kicker, Jon Webb, receives particular attention to his hamstrings and calves from Murph, the physio.

'Good kicking legs,' observes Murph. 'Well-developed hamstrings – what you need.'

'Good legs?' I question incredulously, looking at Jon's pipe-cleaners. 'He had to tie a knot in them to have knees!'

2.25 p.m.

Coach Geoff Cooke enters the room and pours himself a cup of tea from the now lukewarm pot. It has been stewing for so long that, when he pours, it comes out looking like something flushed from a radiator.

'Everybody down in five,' Geoff announces, meaning he wants every one of us seated, changed, quiet and ready to listen to his team talk in five minutes' time.

He takes a sip of his tea and pulls a face that would win a Cumbrian gurning competition. He puts the cup back on the tray. 'Who's responsible for that piss?' he asks assistant John Elliott. John shrugs his shoulders.

'Another ten minutes in there and it will have dissolved that bloody teapot,' grumbles Geoff.

Geoff notices Mike Teague reading the programme. He stands in front of Mike and claps his hands. 'C'mon Teaguey, son, let's have you!'

As if a lightning bolt has suddenly hit him, Mike jumps to his feet. It seems as though he has suddenly been woken from a very deep sleep and is not sure of his whereabouts for a minute or so. Gathering himself, he begins to get ready in double-quick time.

I could do with using one of the loos but they are in constant demand.

2.27 p.m.

The referee enters to check our studs and tell us that he doesn't want to see anyone 'being funny out there'. 'Pity Little and Large aren't playing, then,' says Mike Teague.

We all laugh, glad of the relief from the tension.

We all raise our feet so that the referee can run a hand across our studs to check for jagged edges that might inflict injury. He nods to captain Will Carling to indicate all is well. 'Good luck, lads,' he says as he leaves.

'And you, ref,' we all chorus.

2.30 p.m.

Geoff Cooke has been through everything the day before, so his pre-match talk is more of a reminder of the main points of our game plan. He goes over our tactics for the line-outs, particularly the calls. He refers to scrummaging and 'channel one', where we will attempt to feed the ball at lightning speed through the legs of loose head, between number 8 and flanker to Richard Hill at scrum-half, who then will look for Rory Underwood coming up from deep. 'We need quick ball today,' Geoff tells us.

Geoff reminds us of channels two, three and four, the other ways we are to move the ball through the scrum. He then outlines what is expected in the rucks and mauls and ends with words of encouragement.

'You're here because you are the best there are,' he tells us. 'Go out and show them just how good you are. Enjoy yourselves, and remember, you can never win too much ball.'

He wishes us good luck and exits in search of a hot, preferably fresh, cup of tea.

2.40 p.m.

Captain Will Carling is more abrasive, direct and emotional in his talk. He starts slowly, then begins to wind us up and motivate us until we are getting frenzied.

'Let's get stuck into these right from the start. Let them know they're in a 'king game from the word go,' says Will. 'Win our personal battles against our opposite numbers and we'll win out there today.'

We all nod. Studs start to be stamped on the floor.

'Let's run them so much that in the last ten minutes, they're breathing through their arses.'

Will builds his captain's talk so that it ends on a climactic note. 'Let's go! Let's go! Let's go! We're winners!' he shouts as we all jump to our feet.

I join some players in stretching exercises. Others sprint on the spot. Brian Moore is gritting his teeth and hitting his face hard with the palm of his right hand. Jon Webb is taking long, deep breaths. Will Carling swings his arms to touch his right toes with his left hand, then his left toes with his right hand. Mike Teague's eyes have disappeared deep into their sockets. He makes little jolting motions with his chin and wiggles his arms by his sides. His face is inscrutable. Wade Dooley is staring blankly in silence at the door.

2.50 p.m.

There is a knock on the door. The referee's whistle blows and a steward out in the corridor swings the door open. We all wish one another luck, shake hands, pat each other on the back or backside.

I hang around for a moment. The team leaves the dressing room in crocodile fashion and I must be second from the end of the line. I squeeze between Rob Andrew and Mike Teague, who is always last out.

The floor of the corridor is protected from our studs by rubberised matting. As we turn to head down the tunnel it sounds as if hundreds of tappets from a car engine have got out of synch. We make a hell of a racket as we clitter-clatter down the tunnel heading towards the rectangle of light at the end.

The crowd on the opposite side erupt as they see Will Carling emerge first. The area of light is getting bigger. More cheers as more of the crowd react to seeing the team. The area of light seems to be even bigger than the width of the tunnel. A cacophonous roar rings around the stadium by the time Will is five steps on to the pitch. I dive into the light. A wall of sound assaults my ears. My heart is thumping so heavily and so quickly I half expect the people in the crowd to notice. My boots hit the soft green turf and I sprint five or so yards, more to rid myself of pent-up energy than anything else.

I look up and around the stands. There are thousands and thousands of heads. I've never seen so many heads. Brown hair, black hair, heads with caps. They look so still, they can't be responsible for all this noise, surely?

Wade Dooley calls to me. I look across to him and he throws me a ball. I catch it. It muddies my hands. I pass it on to Rob Andrew. I rub the palms of my hands on the turf then wipe them on my shirt front. I spit into both palms and rub them together. It warms my hands and, more importantly, makes them tacky.

I look up the field and see the opposition. They are passing balls among themselves, apparently oblivious to the crowd and us. It's as if they are having their own private training session and, once it is over, they will leave the field.

The referee and touch-judges appear. Will Carling gets the signal to call us over to line up for the national anthems. Both teams form one long line facing the main stand. From somewhere over my right shoulder a band has struck up the first bar of 'God Save the Queen'. I mouth and at best mumble the words. It is like being in church – I feel self-conscious about the fact that someone may hear me singing. A ridiculous notion in front of a crowd of 68,000.

The anthems over, the captains join the match officials in the centre of the pitch. I wander downfield to take up my position. I'm not feeling comfortable. My shorts are too tight. The laces in my boots have worked themselves too slack. They'll come undone and I'll have to retie them. I debate whether to do them up again now to save me doing it later.

I'm wearing swimming trunks under my shorts and they start to itch and irritate. My breathing gets quicker and more shallow. Will Carling trots back to take up his position. I wonder why on earth the back of my neck picks this moment to feel so tight and I look up to see the opposing full-back preparing to kick off.

3.00 p.m.

I rub the palm of my right hand across my brow to remove the sweat. When I glance down at my hand, there is no sweat on it whatsoever.

He's kicked it. I find myself running forwards to meet the ball. From now on it's in the lap of the gods.

Tours

'We were so fired up, when the referee ran on to the pitch, three of us tackled him.'

Graham Dawe, Bath and England.

'I said to the manager, this is supposed to be a five-star hotel and there's a bloody hole in the roof. He turned around and said, "That's where you can see the five stars from." '

Gordon Brown, West of Scotland, Scotland and British Lions.

19

Tour De Force

Representing your country at any sport at any level is an honour. To play for England on tour, however, is extra special because you are in a foreign country and in many respects you are not only a player but an ambassador for England.

Like anything else, touring with England has its plusses and minuses. Staying in a five-star hotel in Fiji that affords balcony views of a turquoise sea is wonderful. Sharing a room with someone who expects you to be in bed by ten o'clock every night and tries to convince you that being an auditor is a fascinating job is not so hot. I've always believed auditors are people who turned away from accountancy because they found it too exciting.

My first trip abroad with England wasn't a tour in the true sense of the word because it was to Australia for the first Rugby World Cup in 1987.

I knew that as an England player you were given a tour blazer and tie but was somewhat taken aback to find we were also given flannels, shirts, socks, shoes and underpants! 'Tour underpants?' I remember thinking to myself disbelievingly.

The clothes were handed out at the pre-tour briefing held in a Twickenham hotel a week before our departure. One of the RFU officials responsible for handing out jackets and flannels stood shouting, 'Jacket and trousers! Jacket and trousers!' at the top of his voice as if he were selling the damn things in a market.

As I reported to the hotel with Jon Webb, the two of us could hear this official shouting as we entered the lobby.

'Who on earth is that?' asked Webby.

'Sounds like a man in a loud suit!' I said.

When you embark on tour, you are given a tour itinerary which, in addition to detailing all the games that are to be played, gives a list of the hotels where you will be staying with their phone and fax numbers so that family and friends can contact you.

When we set off for the 1987 World Cup only one hotel was listed. 'There's only one hotel listed on my itinerary,' I pointed out to Dudley Wood, the secretary of the RFU.

'That's right. We're only staying in the one,' Dudley informed me.

'For a whole month?' I inquired incredulously.

Sure enough, we spent the entire month in our allocated rooms in the same hotel. We played games in Sydney and Brisbane, but we didn't leave that hotel to stay elsewhere by way of a break, not even for a couple of days.

After a month sitting in the same room looking at the same four walls and that damn picture of the Sydney Harbour Bridge and Opera House your mind starts to go.

From the window of the room I shared with Richard Hill we had an uninterrupted view of a church with a billboard sign by its entrance. The billboard was used for posters that conveyed what the clergy obviously thought were very witty, poignant, hip religious messages designed to encourage people to attend the church. The message changed every day.

Every morning I used to get up first and look out of the

window to check the weather, though heaven knows why, because it was always sunny. Every day Richard would lie there and ask what that day's gem from the church was. 'Fight truth decay, brush up your Bible every day,' I said, reading the poster.

Every morning I'd stand by the window and pull the curtain to one side as usual. 'Come in for a faith lift!' I reported to Richard.

'You sound like Julian Clary,' he replied. The next morning: 'Come to our "C", "H", then it's got asterisk, asterisk, then the letters "C" and "H" again.'

'Come to our church. What's missing? U R!' Richard groaned and pulled a pillow over his head.

And so we continued, Richard and I, living life in a room that was turning into a cell, living our very own Groundhog Day every day.

'Seven prayerless days make one spiritually weak!'

'Not bad,' said Richard, sitting up and slowly clapping his hands.

The next day: 'Sing a hymn for HIM!'

'Nowhere near as good as the last one,' was Richard's opinion.

The day after that: 'It's impossible to lose your footing on your knees!'

'Enough! Enough! I can't take this any more!' Richard screamed, hands over his ears as he rushed into the bathroom. In truth neither could I.

A year later I was back in Australia with the England touring party. It was during this particular tour that I found out just how two-faced and hypocritical some of the RFU officials could be.

We were playing at the Concord Oval in Sydney against New South Wales. It had been raining incessantly for twenty-four hours and the pitch was like the Somme. As you ran you almost lost your boots because of the suction caused by the six inches of mud that made you feel you were playing on molasses.

In the previous games Jeff Probyn from Wasps had been in the side but he had not done well in the scrummaging, so I came into the team for this merry jaunt against one of Australia's top state sides. I'd done well in the 'Wednesday' side, more or less equivalent to the second XV on tour, and against New South Wales Alan Davies, who went on to coach Wales, had given me the job of keeping the scrum locked. I must have done well because after the game he said, 'Well done,' and told me the scrum had moved 'about as far as Nelson's Column has moved in recent years'.

You don't need anyone to tell you when you've had a good or bad game, you know it yourself. Put in a really bad performance and the coach won't need to say you have been poor. The guy playing behind you will already have told you!

Against New South Wales I felt good because I knew I'd achieved what had been asked of me. I felt I had done particularly well because I'd been propping against a mountain of a man who had the strength of a couple of dray horses. His name was Peter Kay.

Among other things Peter Kay, a former Hell's Angel, had worked as a bouncer on the door of a brothel in King's Cross, the red-light district of Sydney. The stories that circulated about him would make my hair stand on end — if I had any. At an official function a few days before the game the Australian scrum-half, Nick Farr-Jones, told me that one night four sailors tried to crash the brothel where Peter Kay worked. He took on all four at once and beat the hell out of them, then coolly wandered into the snooker room, where he shot a break of 122.

I started to feel edgy and wary.

'Now, come on, Nick, that is a bit of an exaggeration,' David Campese said, much to my relief. 'That break was only ninety-eight!'

Throughout the game I had been engaged in a ding-dong battle with the gargantuan Kay. When the final whistle blew I started to walk towards the main grandstand, shaking hands with opponents on the way. I was only about three yards from the touchline, right in front of the seated officials from both sides, when Peter Kay approached me.

I extended a hand. At first it looked as if he were about to shake hands as well. Instead he wound up a fist the size of a demolition ball and tried to send me into the arms of Morpheus. Luckily I saw it coming and managed to take evasive action before grabbing him and putting him on the floor. I ended up sitting on him, threatening to run him up the biggest dental bill in history, while the press boys buzzed around us like hover flies getting their photographs.

Players from both sides intervened and, as Wade Dooley and Dean Richards pulled me away, Kay's team-mates propelled him towards the dressing room.

As we sat drinking our tea in the changing room we received the news that Peter Kay had been included in the Australian side for the second Test. As they say Down Under, 'the selectors liked the cut of his jib'. It was his first cap. As it turned out, it was to be his only one. The Australian selectors were for a time cock-a-hoop about Kay, as they felt he showed the aggression and bottle necessary to take on the Poms. Although I didn't relish coming up against him again, I certainly wasn't worried about it. If the Australian selectors thought I would be intimidated by him, they had another think coming. Later that evening I was summoned to an emergency meeting of the RFU tour officials. I was told I wouldn't be picked for the second Test after all. Peter Kay had been picked for Australia and they feared 'a confrontation'.

I was told that my conduct at the end of the game, in front of the main grandstand and press cameras, was such that I could count myself damned lucky I wasn't on the next plane home.

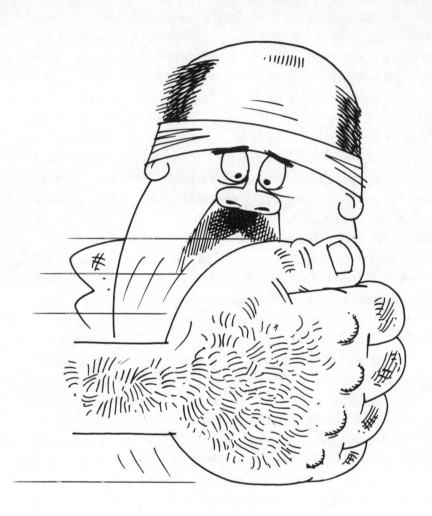

The difference in the attitude between the English and the Australian selectors was unbelievable. That said, it came as no real surprise; it was par for the course. The RFU selectors have always been hypocritical. In international rugby we have seen disgraceful thuggery from the French front rows and body-damaging stamping from the All Blacks. But I was 'lucky' not to be sent home for wrestling to the ground a brute who had tried to break my jaw when I had extended a hand of friendship to him!

The coach at the time, Alan Davies, gave me about as much support as a threadbare jockstrap. When asked about the incident he told the press of me, 'I can't see how he can play again on this tour after that.'

Sour grapes on my part? Compare my treatment to that meted out to Northampton's Tim Rodber, who was sent off for violent play during the England tour of South Africa in 1994. The press felt that Tim, an officer in the army, should have exercised restraint. In the furore that followed his dismissal the media and rugby fans were saying that Tim should be hauled over the coals for his behaviour. Many wanted him sent home and banned. What did the selectors do? They picked him for the next Test.

I told the chairman of the disciplinary hearing that I had not instigated the scuffle with Kay. For that's all it was. I had behaved as any reasonable person would have done when attacked. The chairman told me I should have let Kay hit me and not retaliated. 'Do you know what a man wants to be when he takes it on the chin like that, Chilcott?' he asked.

'Dead?' I inquired.

20

Lion Heart

S OME SO-CALLED rugby pundits have called for an end to British Lions tours, the argument being that, with the Courage Leagues, Pilkington Cup, Five Nations, individual RU summer tours and a World Cup every four years, there is simply too much competitive rugby. Ask any top-class player, however, and he will tell you that the Lions must continue.

It is every player's dream to be part of a Lions' tour. To be chosen is the pinnacle of a playing career, and there is a camaraderie and team spirit that is unique to the Lions.

When the top thirty players from the home countries are chosen for the Lions squad, they face a real test of character. They immediately have to become friends and team-mates of those they have already battled against in the intense atmosphere of rivalry of the Five Nations Championship. During a Lions tour no two players from one country are allowed to room with one another and the integration is extended by having forwards and backs rooming together.

Those who want to see an end to Lions tours are talking nonsense. If they feel that there are too many competitive games they should get rid of the Divisional games, for a start, and take a fresh look at the whole playing structure of rugby.

Those North-West versus Midlands representative games are a waste of time. If you need proof of that, look at how many of the top players make excuses for not playing in them.

The thought of the England soccer manager calling for a London versus North-East representative game so that he can make up his mind whether or not a Newcastle United or Arsenal player is up to the mark for the national team is unthinkable. So why should it be different for rugby? The RFU selectors are watching players in Courage League One every week, for heaven's sake. Why can't they select a team on the basis of that?

The British Lions' most recent tour was in 1993 to New Zealand, where they lost the series 2–1. The one drawback to touring is that the referees are usually local and can easily be intimidated and swayed. Touring sides in Great Britain enjoy neutral referees but it does not stop the All Blacks bending the rules. They do this basically in four different ways. In line-outs, as soon as the ball is thrown, they close the one-metre gap between the teams, which protects their throw and disrupts their opponents'. In rucks and mauls they step over the top to cause obstruction. On attack, kicking or running, they put defenders as blockers between you and the ball – obstruction yet again.

Just as the Aussie cricketers have 'sledging', the All Blacks have 'blagging'. They shout constantly at the referee and can 'blag' an official relatively inexperienced at international level into thinking he is out of his depth. If the official is weak and you don't exert your own presence, they can end up 'refereeing' the game.

The 1993 Lions tour, like the 1989 one to Australia in which I took part, was soured not only by some dubious refereeing but also by an itinerary that was far too demanding on the players. Those 1993 Lions had only one day off in the whole of a three-month tour – and that was the day after the final Test.

That tour also gained notoriety for the grossly insensitive treatment of the Preston Grasshoppers forward Wade Dooley. The tour was supposed to be his swansong before his retirement after nine glorious years of international rugby. In New Zealand he received the sad news that his father had died and he had to fly home. The Lions tour officials told him he could rejoin the party at a later date. Little did he know that, as he flew back to England, his replacement was being flown out.

When the time came for Wade to return, he was told that he couldn't because there was no money in the budget for his air fare or hotels. The All Blacks, on hearing this, sportingly had a whip-round and raised the air fare. However, tour officials told Wade he could not accept the money as it would be viewed as payment. Furthermore, an International Rugby Board directive did not allow for one 'extra' man in the touring party. Again the All Blacks said they had no objection to the Lions having one player more than the allocated thirty, but the IRB stood firm.

In the end he was told he could rejoin the Lions and train with them but that he would not be allowed to play. There seemed little point in this, so Wade decided to stay at home – hardly a fitting finale for a man who had literally sweated blood for England and Great Britain.

On hearing of Wade's plight the New Zealand public felt badly about the way he had been treated. There was a lot of bitterness towards the International Rugby Board and certain Lions tour officials, whom they believed had been totally insensitive. This feeling was epitomised at a dinner held to honour the Lions in Auckland.

Bob Weighill, the secretary of the Lions tour party, allegedly asked a waiter placing knobs of butter on individual side plates for a second pat of butter to accompany his bread roll.

'I'm sorry sir, chef's orders. One pat of butter per person,' the waiter told Weighill.

'Don't be silly, man. One more pat of butter is not going to make a difference. Put it on my plate.'

Again the waiter refused, much to Weighill's annoyance and the acute embarrassment of officials and players from both sides who were seated nearby. Weighill tried a third time but the waiter was adamant. One pat of butter per person. Weighill was now furious. 'Do you know who I am?' he asked, now beetroot-faced.

'No, sir.'

'I am Bob Weighill, chairman of the Harlequins Rugby Football Club! Chairman of the England selection committee! And secretary, and, therefore, to all intents and purposes, in charge of this British Lions tour!' he said indignantly.

'And do you know who I am?' asked the waiter.

'No.'

'I'm in charge of the butter.'

21

Wizard Time in Oz
With Not So Timid Lions

THERE IS no grey area as far as Lions tours are concerned. Like the little girl with the curl, they are either very, very good or very, very bad.

Even though the home countries selectors may, to their mind, have chosen the best thirty players in the British Isles to make up a Lions touring party, it is not always guaranteed that the rugby will be of the very best quality. Sometimes the players gel, sometimes they do not. The style of play adopted on that particular tour may not suit a number of the players' personal styles. The players themselves may not form friendships and, when backs are against the wall, are you really going to put your head on the line for someone who is unsociable towards you?

I was lucky – the 1989 British Lions tour to Australia was a highly successful one. Australia were considered, along with New Zealand, to be the best rugby side in the world at the time and to go out there and win the Test series 2–1 gave us enormous satisfaction. What made the achievement all the more remarkable was the fact we lost the first Test in Sydney by 30–12. We bounced back in Brisbane, winning 19–12, and in the final Test, back in Sydney, held out against a Herculean late onslaught by the Aussies to win 19–18.

I'm a great admirer of the Australians. Whatever code of rugby they play, and in cricket, they always manage to replace a very good side with yet another very good one. For two nations who are so friendly to one another, the competitiveness on the field between British teams and the Aussies is always red-hot, irrespective of the sport. That is why I took great satisfaction as the final whistle blew in that third Test in seeing the Australian lads stagger away, bewildered and defeated like vanquished soldiers limping away from the field of battle.

We'd maintained a proud Lions record of never having lost a series in Australia except, that is, when they first toured there in 1930, and one can hardly call that a series since only one Test match was played. Essential to our success was the fact that, as people, all the players got on very well indeed. No one spoiled the happy family atmosphere, although towards the end of the tour Bridgend's Mike Griffiths had irritated so many of us we began to call him Thrush.

What makes Lions tours so engaging and attractive to top players is their scarcity. As they take place every four to six years – sometimes not even for eight years – they have to coincide with a player being at his peak performance-wise. I know of dozens of players who longed to tour with the Lions. They were good enough but the tours didn't happen when they were playing their best rugby. It is this rarity value, like that of truffles in a wood or a good joke in a *Little and Large Show*, that makes Lions tours so highly prized. The management team on this tour comprised Clive Rowlands, who was team manager; Ian McGeechan, assistant manager and coach; and Roger Uttley, assistant coach. Together they worked extremely well and formed a good blend. Ian was not the best motivator in the world, but Roger was. Conversely, Roger's technical ability as a coach at that level was not good, whereas Ian showed himself as one of the best coaches in top-class rugby.

Following his success as coach of Scotland, during which time they won the Grand Slam in 1990, Ian McGeechan was appointed coach at Courage League One side Northampton in 1994. After his first coaching session at Franklins Gardens he felt a twinge of pain in his right knee, an old injury caused by too much twisting and turning at speed during an illustrious playing career with Leeds-based Headingley and Scotland, for whom he won thirty-two caps. Ian set off in search of the club physio, hoping to get some heat treatment. When he entered the physio's room only the club captain, Tim Rodber, was there.

'Do you have anything for this old rugby knee?' asked Ian, pointing to his right patella.

'Only the greatest of respect,' replied Tim.

During this tour we visited quite a number of sheep farms and our captain, Stewart's-Melville's Finlay Calder, marvelled at how many ex-pat Scots were out in Oz running them. The fact that we had great Scottish players such as Gavin and Scott Hastings, John Jeffrey, Peter Dods, Craig Chalmers and David Sole on tour with us really brought out the farmers' patriotism and they often welcomed us on our visits bedecked in full highland costume, kilt and all.

'It brings a tear to your eye, it really does,' said Finlay as we left one farmer in full national costume. 'They must still really love Scotland to be out here and wearing the kilt.'

'Bugger that,' Mike Teague retorted as he boarded the coach. 'They only wear kilts out here because the sheep have got used to the noise of a zip.'

We played a number of games in what we referred to as 'the territories'. We'd fly for hours and not see any trace of mankind; then, suddenly, rising out of the outback would be a lone town such as Oodnadatta in South Australia or Cooktown on the Cape York Peninsula in northern Queensland.

From our Sydney base we flew over the Blue Mountains to Dubbo in New South Wales, a busy junction town for road, rail and air traffic. The land around Dubbo is some of the richest and most fertile agricultural land in Australia, and the town's transport links were established to ship the varied produce west to Sydney and to Melbourne in the south. Dubbo is a bustling town which produces some surprisingly good rugby sides, considering that the population is only around 25,000 and the place itself quite isolated.

On the coach from the airport to the Dubbo rugby ground Paul Ackford piped up: 'They're an odd lot out here, you know. The family trees have no branches to them.'

I nodded and smiled but Bob Norster, sitting next to me, wasn't with Paul on this one at all.

'How d'you mean?' he asked, his face screwed up in puzzlement.

'I mean they're all inter-bred out here,' said Paul.

'What? You mean they're all bakers?' asked Bob as he turned to gaze out of the coach window at mile after mile of wheatfields.

We won the game comfortably enough, by 39–6. During the post-match reception for players and officials, Mike Teague and I were entranced by one of the Dubbo officials. To say he was of striking appearance is to put it mildly. He had the physique of a lamp-post and stood almost as tall. The features of a thin, drawn face pointed down to an enormous bulbous chin that would not have been out of place on Desperate Dan. The chin looked grossly incongruous on such a tapering face. The other striking aspect was his teeth. Not just two but three of his front teeth bulged from under his upper lip, giving his face a permanent dopey, sneering smile.

'He looks like he's got three Beechnuts wedged under that top lip,' said Mike as we tried not to make our attention too evident. He called Bob Norster over.

'See that official over there, Bob?' asked Mike, pointing him out.

'Bloody hell!' said an astonished Bob. 'He's a queer-looking bugger if ever I saw one.'

'Yes, well let that be a lesson to you,' said Mike, nodding towards the official in question. 'That's what happens when cousins marry.'

If it had not been for physiotherapist Kevin Murphy, I would not have played much rugby on the tour at all. I damaged the calf muscle on my right leg early on and it was only Kevin's daily attention for the entire two-and-a-half months of the tour that kept me a player rather than a supporter. Such was Kevin's daily devotion, he told me, that towards the end of the tour he used to see my right leg every night in his sleep. One billion women in the world and Kevin gets to dream about my right leg. Some people have no luck at all.

Whenever the Lions or a national side go touring, two committees are immediately formed by the players. One is really a jury that sits in judgment of fellow players who have committed minor misdemeanours or 'spoof' offences – such as Judge Paul Rendall sentencing Scott Hastings to listen to two hours of Richard Clayderman tapes on his personal stereo after being found guilty of having his hair cut in a style that was 'an affront to what little hair Graham Dawe had left'. The other is the entertainment committee, whose job it is to organise games, visits and other activities for the players' 'free time'. On this Lions tour I was on the entertainment committee. After training sessions in the morning we organised all manner of surprisingly sensible and healthy pursuits. Sailing, surfing, windsurfing, tennis, table tennis, cricket – even cinema and theatre visits.

I ended up going to see my first opera. We had a free night to spend as we pleased. Gavin Hastings, Rob Andrew and Ieuan Evans said they were 'off to *La Traviata*' and would I like to come? It wouldn't cost me anything as they'd been given complimentary tickets. I thought they were going to an Italian spaghetti house, so I said yes.

As one who always thought Caruso was one of the Marx Brothers, attending an opera was a unique experience for me. When the prima donna hit a high note I applauded, I didn't know she still had thirty-two bars to go. The opera fascinated me. It is the only art form I know where, when the main character is killed, he starts singing.

Of course, there were many 'off-the-wall' entertainments organised. These usually involved consuming copious amounts of alcohol at some stage, such as on the night after the second Test at Ballymore in Brisbane.

The Australians had the rub of the green in the first Test in Sydney. We had allowed them to dictate the style of play and we knew that in the second Test we had to gain the upper hand and 'boss' the game. The match itself was very physical and for the most part tight. There wasn't a lot between the two sides. In such circumstances you look to your gifted and skilled players to pull something special out of the bag as only they can. In this game it was Jerry Guscott who produced it, weaving in and out of flaying hands during a mazy run before sprinting home for the winning try. Mike Teague was outstanding that day and ended up being voted Player of the Series, a well-deserved accolade.

That night in the team hotel during a break from one of our celebration drinking games, David Sole was accompanying me to the bar to help ferry drinks when he thought he recognised someone from his Edinburgh days.

'Hello there!' said a swaying David. 'What brings you over to Oz?'

The guy looked David up and down and it was clear to me that he'd never seen him before in his life. 'I live here,' he said

in a noticeable Brisbane accent.

'Didn't you used to have a beard at one time?' asked David as I busied the barman with our drinks order.

'Me? No, never,' said the man, smiling at David's inebriated condition.

'You've shrunk. You used to be taller,' slurred David. 'And you've lost weight. Lost a lot of weight, you have.'

The man looked at me, nodded towards David and laughed at the case of mistaken identity.

'Here, take these,' I said, putting an end to the stranger's embarrassment by handing David a tray of drinks. I paid the barman and took the other tray of beers. 'Come on you,' I said to David and nodded towards where the rest of the players were sitting.

'Anyway, nice to see you again, Mr Forsyth,' said David, smiling through his alcoholic haze.

'And my name is not Forsyth,' called the man as we carried the drinks back to our tables.

Half-way across the room, David leaned into me. 'He's changed his bloody name as well.'

22

Donal's Doughnuts

ON ANY major rugby tour there will be two teams, a Saturday and a Wednesday side, the former being the potential best XV. The Wednesday side, as the name suggests, plays midweek as opposed to at weekends and, to all intents and purposes, acts as a second XV, though you are apt to find that just about every player in the squad will have played for both sides come the end of a tour.

During the 1989 tour of Australia the Wednesday team acquired the nickname of Donal's Doughnuts – Doughnuts because they played to 'fill the whole in the middle of the week', and Donal's because they were captained by the great Cork Constitution forward Donal Lenihan.

Donal is one of the greatest rugby forwards ever to come out of Ireland. In an international career that stretched from 1981 to 1992, he won fifty-two caps for Ireland and was a key member of their Triple Crown sides of 1982 and 1985. It is no coincidence that Donal had an outstanding game when Ireland recorded their highest ever score and greatest margin of victory in an international, 60–0 against Romania in Dublin in 1986. Nor that, when Donal did not play against New Zealand in 1992, the Irish were beaten 59–6, their heaviest international defeat. Donal gave teams an inspired leadership. At 6ft 7, with blue eyes and a handsome moustache, Donal looked more like a Boston Celtic basketball player than a rugby player from County Cork. A product of University College, Cork, he is a highly intelligent man with a sharp wit that instantly cuts you to the bone.

In one morning training session during the 1989 Lions tour Donal set out a number of traffic cones. The idea was that we'd sprint between them but they seemed too close to one another to allow us to weave in and out with any degree of comfort.

Bridgend's Mike Griffiths eyed the closeness of the cones. 'Can I ask a stupid question?'

'Better than anyone I know,' said Donal, quick as a flash.

On another occasion we were driving through Sydney on our way to a function hosted by the Australian RFU when we passed a couple coming out of a church after being married.

'Why do people throw rice at weddings?' asked Jerry Guscott, in all earnestness.

'Because rocks hurt,' retorted Donal immediately.

When Scott Hastings remarked that his brother Gavin seemed to prefer playing tennis or going windsurfing with Ieuan Evans rather than with him, Donal put it in perspective for him. 'Ieuan's like the brother Gavin never had,' he said.

'What about me?' asked Scott.

'You're the brother he did have,' said Donal.

It was all good-humoured and never meant or taken personally. The camaraderie on that Australian tour was first-class. If we had not all been pulling for one another, there is no way it would have been such a successful series.

Donal also proved on this tour that he possessed a constitution like steel. He led from the front during games, and afterwards he led from the front into every single Irish Guinness bar in Australia.

On one such expedition, on a rare night off after a tough

and arduous 27–11 victory over Australian Capital Territories, we celebrated by quenching our thirsts with ice-cold Guinness in every bar we could find in Canberra. Come three in the morning the rain was lashing down as we spilled out on to the pavement from the Friends of Ireland bar. Everyone's legs, except those belonging to Donal, had a mind of their own. Rubber-limbed, we staggered around trying to make major decisions, such as establishing the direction our hotel was in, and getting a thorough soaking for our sins. As the priest who had been our host bade us farewell, Andy Robinson was so far gone that he told the father he was wearing his collar back to front.

'I'm a father, Andrew,' said the priest.

'I've got kids myself,' said Andy, swaying like a tree in a stiff breeze.

'No, I am the father to hundreds of people in this area,' explained the priest, smiling benignly.

'Really?' said Andy, taken aback. 'In that case, it's not your collar you should be wearing back to front, it's your bloody trousers!'

Thoroughly soaked and tired, to a man all we wanted to do was get back to our hotel and crash out into our beds. Donal, however, was having none of it. Belying his consumption of fifteen or so pints of Guinness, Donal stood upright and calm, hands in pockets, as he listened to our pleas to be taken home.

'No, lads,' he said, shaking his head slowly. 'Surely not. The night is but a pup.'

In answer to our prayers Brian Moore told us he had worked out how to get back to our hotel and we all gratefully followed in his wake. By then Andy Robinson was totally out of it, lying prostrate on his back in a puddle in the road as the rain continued unabated. He proved he was a lost cause when he started to fling his arms out and shout: 'Save the women and children first. I can swim!'

As the rest of us followed Brian to our hotel I glanced back to see Donal gently lifting Andy from the roadside, placing him gently across his shoulder and striding purposefully off in the opposite direction in search of an all-night bar that sold Guinness.

With his doughnuts safely tucked up in bed, Donal visited another three bars, drinking his Guinness and carrying a comatose Andy across his shoulder the entire time.

The next day a very fragile Andy Robinson received a telephone call from a girl to whom he had apparently been chatting the night before. Such had been Andy's condition that he couldn't even remember the girl, never mind giving her the hotel telephone number. He took the call while we were having lunch and diplomatically managed to sidestep the issue.

'Can't remember talking to her at all,' he said, resuming his place at the dining table. 'I managed to get rid of her, thank heavens. If the wife found out I'd been chatting up the girls she'd kill me.'

'Now, would you know, that's the Guinness for you,' said Donal, as he stretched back in his chair, meal completed. 'It always makes you English boys see double and feel single.'

That victory over Australian Capital Territories was an important one as far as the tour was concerned. Having lost the first Test heavily it was important that we, as a team, bounced back with a convincing result to restore confidence and morale. No one likes to lose a vital game early on in a tour, even if excuses can be made for acclimatisation, effects of jet-lag and what have you. Australian Capital Territories were seen as a very strong outfit, so not only to beat them but to beat them well did us the power of good. It told the Aussies that we meant business.

Australian Capital Territories, or ACT for short, comprises

ten clubs and is ranked as one of the top three rugby states in Australia. The teams that form the ACT state league have the sort of names that appear to have been made up by a screenwriter penning a nineteenth-century Australian bodice-ripper. Captain's Flat, Gundaroo, Bungendore, Ginnindera and Queanbeyan. I've always wondered if the latter was really Aussie for Queen Bee? The names may appear humorous to us Poms but ACT has produced some great players over the years, notably the incomparable David Campese.

I hadn't played in that first Test, but Ian McGeechan brought me into the side for this game at the Canberra Rangers Stadium against ACT to form a front-row partnership with Steve Smith of Ireland and Mike Griffiths of Wales.

After five minutes came the first line-out. As Donal jumped for the ball, Bob O'Connor, all 6ft 8ins of him, elbowed him out of the line. Cheekbone swelling like a balloon, Donal gave me his first captain's instruction of the game. 'Coochie! I want that 'king big goon sorted!'

Next line-out all 5ft 10 of me leaped against the lofty O'Connor. With my right fist I hit him with everything I could muster. O'Connor never moved a muscle. In fact, Swansea's Robert Jones told me afterwards, the bastard smiled!

The rest of the game continued in that vein, with me hitting O'Connor only for O'Connor to hit me back. At the final whistle both of us staggered off the pitch as if we were John Wayne and Victor McLaglen after their running fight in John Ford's film *The Quiet Man*. Donal Lenihan, however, left the pitch skipping with joy. Not only had he captained us to a famous victory, he'd had so much of the ball he'd been given the Man of the Match Award.

After the game Donal and I were propping up the bar. In Donal's case he was simply relaxing; I, on the other hand, was using the bar for much-needed support for my aching body. It had been such a battle with O'Connor I even had bruises on my bruises. Donal sipped his Guinness and stared across the room to the lumbering and cumbersome frame of O'Connor as, slack-jawed, he patrolled the room behaving like an oaf.

'To be sure, it's fascinating is it not?' Donal said.

'What is?'

He nodded in the direction of O'Connor. 'That twenty-six years ago, out of 10,000 sperm, he was the quickest!'

23

Go East, Young Man

I F I were to ask you which country lays claim to having the most rugby clubs, I don't imagine many would say Japan. But it has.

Travel, they say, should broaden the mind. It certainly broadened mine. Take Japan. Before going there I never realised just how big rugby is in that beautiful country. The fact that there are so many club sides is astounding because finding land for pitches is a real problem, not to mention expensive. In 1995 land in Tokyo itself cost £2 million an acre.

Given that they are not the tallest people in the world, which in itself precludes certain styles of play, and given their geographical isolation in rugby terms, together with their colossal facility problem, the Japanese have coped with all their disadvantages remarkably well and in the true spirit of the game. The RFU were delighted when a crowd of 68,000 turned up at Twickenham to see Bath beat Leicester 21–9 to clinch the Pilkington Cup in 1994. The finals of the Pilkington Cup, and its predecessor, the John Player Cup, had regularly drawn disappointing attendances considering that they are the showpiece of the season.

The Japanese could never understand this. Their cup final,

between the club champions and the university champions, always attracts between 55,000 and 65,000 spectators. The 68,000 that turned up at Twickenham in 1994 set a new world record for a club match attendance. What few realise is that the previous record was held by the Japanese for the 66,000 who turned up for their 1990 cup final.

Some rugby pundits condescendingly refer to Japan as 'one of the developing rugby nations'. Some development! The first game there took place in 1874 and both club and university games attract four- and five-figure attendances.

That said, Japan has in recent years had some wildly extreme results, none more so than in 1987 when, after losing 106–4 to a New Zealand XV, they bounced back to beat Sri Lanka 108–0!

It is by touring such countries as Japan and playing host to touring nations ourselves that we can, I feel, foster a better understanding of one another as people as well as learning about each other's countries in rugby terms.

Whether it be Japan, Australia, Canada, Argentina or Fiji, I love touring. The total amount of money I take on tour I divide by the number of days the tour is to last. That way I ensure I don't run out half-way through. If the team I am with has a day training and then attends an official function that does not necessitate spending any money, I count that as a bonus day in terms of my tour funds. By the same token, if I spend more than my daily allocation, I know I'll have to reduce it the following day to claw back the difference.

Obviously players' circumstances vary, so the amount of money a player takes on tour varies. The most extraordinary example of this I encountered was on the 1989 British Lions tour of Australia.

The Lions squad assembled at a hotel in Middlesex before the flight. As we sat relaxing in the lounge bar, about to depart for a tour Down Under that would last for all of three months,

John Jeffrey, the great Kelso and Scotland forward, ambled up to me. 'I'm taking forty-five quid. That should be enough, shouldn't it, Coochie?' he asked.

'Yes,' I said, gaping, 'as long as you're prepared to live like Gandhi.'

John, however, proved something of an entrepreneur. When he landed in Australia he bought a job-lot of plain white T-shirts and got everyone in the squad to sign each one. He then sold them outside the grounds and in sports shops wherever we went. The venture was so successful for John that he put £450 in the players' beer kitty, lived the life of Riley during the tour and went home with just under £600 in his pocket. People like John Jeffrey should be running the country.

Players are given a daily allowance when on tour with England. When I toured this was in the region of £20 a day, which I considered good. 'How often would I get through twenty quid in a day?' I thought to myself. I had an eye-opener, however, one night in Sydney after we had beaten Japan 60–7 in the World Cup. I wandered into a salubrious Sydney hotel, ordered a long, cool lager and was charged just over £5 – and this was in 1987.

'Five quid for a lager?' I said to the man who served me. 'It's a different set of bars you should be behind.'

I liked what I saw of Australia and I liked what I saw of Japan while on tours. Japan is a land of contrasts. High technology and city hustle and bustle sit alongside the genteel tranquillity of traditional Japanese culture. It's a fascinating juxtaposition of lifestyles.

In 1988 England toured Australia and Fiji. On the flight to Fiji I sat back relishing the thought of balmy evenings spent sipping long, cool drinks on a veranda overlooking peaceful tropical gardens; of a life lived at a slower pace, where hummingbirds hovered about jacaranda trees and a turquoise ocean gently lapped long, white, sandy beaches; where the living was easy and, although Daddy might not be rich, Mama sure was good-looking.

'The Fijians are a wonderful people,' I said to Gary Rees, who was sitting next to me on the plane. 'Very peaceful, very loving. But get them out on a rugby pitch and it's a different matter.'

Within five minutes of our arrival at Nadi Airport the gun and rocket fire started. Our landing had coincided with the beginning of a civil war and military coup.

As the gunfire crackled around us, we all took cover by lying on our stomachs in the airport lounge.

'If this is a demonstration of how peaceful and loving they are,' said Gary Rees, lying prostrate next to me as we listened to the sound of mortars in the distance, 'I'd hate to be here when they fall out with each other.'

Happily the trouble was short-lived and, after the newly installed military government guaranteed our safety to the RFU and the British government, we continued the tour, though the atmosphere was tense at times.

In recent years we have seen teams from the South Sea Islands really emerge in world rugby. Fiji have always done well in seven-a-side tournaments. Sevens rugby puts a great emphasis on running and passing the ball, which suits their style. The Fijians were undisputed masters at sevens – until England clinched the inaugural Rugby World Cup Sevens, held in Scotland in 1993, that is.

When it comes to the fifteen-a-side game, however, Fiji do not do as well. It is much more demanding and calls for far more discipline in an individual's play. When they are not allowed to display their natural fluent, open style of play, the Fijians give way to frustration, which leads to ill-disciplined rugby. This resulted in two sendings-off at Twickenham in 1989 when England beat them 58–23.

I've always thought that, should the Fijians ever manage to

harness their marvellous handling skills – and the athleticism, pace and stamina of which both their backs and forwards are capable – to greater aggression, discipline and ball-winning, they would become one of the major forces in world rugby.

Fiji actually comprises over 800 islands in the South Pacific with a total population of around 750,000. There are over 600 rugby clubs, many running two or three teams which play in sub-unions, all of which makes rugby their national sport.

For a people that enjoy what seems a very laid-back lifestyle, Fijians can whip themselves into a terrible frenzy for a major rugby match.

One of the problems European rugby sides have when visiting Fiji is not so much the heat as the humidity. I came out of the shower following England's 25–12 win in Suva and was still towelling myself down two days later. You never seem to be dry. The atmosphere for that game in Suva was as highly charged as a credit card. The Fijian supporters were in volatile mood. The military coup only days before had turned them from normally placid, reasonable people into the Caligulas of the South Seas. They were hyped into a raving mania and pulled wildly at the fencing that surrounded the pitch as we England players took to the field. As we made our way to the centre it was bedlam. Fruit, bottles, coins, stones, anything and everything started to fly over the top of the fences as the police fired shots into the air. And all the time those at the front kept pulling at the wire, apparently in an attempt to bring it down. At one point I was hit on the head by a stone thrown by a spectator who was standing by the tunnel next to the dug-outs. Hardly inconspicuous!

It was almost as if the crowd were possessed as we lined up for the national anthems. They screamed and spat abuse at us and grew more and more aggressive.

'We'll all be lucky to get out of here alive,' I muttered.

'Speak for yourself,' I heard a voice next to me say.

I turned and saw it was Jerry Guscott.

The game itself was a tough, tense affair. Not for one moment did that crowd let up in their aggression and abuse of the England team throughout the game. Then, when the final whistle sounded, the strangest thing happened. The whole atmosphere changed. Not gradually, but immediately, the way the picture on your TV changes when you press the channel-selector handset. Within seconds the Fijians who had been baying for our blood were shaking our hands, saying how well we had played and inviting us to visit them in their homes for a drink.

During the post-match buffet a Fijian supporter came up and asked me for my autograph. He went on to ask if I would like to return with him to his home for a drink and to meet his family. I recognised him as the supporter who had stood near the tunnel and thrown the stone that had hit me on the head.

'You're the one who hit me on the head with a stone!' I said, somewhat miffed.

'Now, what you go frettin' 'bout that for, Mr Chilcott,' he said, smiling. 'Dat der stone was only on your 'ead for a split-second, man!'

Fitness, Tactics and Training

'If you broke Chilcott's arm he'd kick you. If you broke his leg he'd bite you. And if you took all his teeth out he would headbutt you.'

Nick Farr-Jones, New South Wales and Australia.

'Geoff Cooke said that when he was finished with me I'd be fit to drop. I was and he did.'

Dewi Morris, Orrell, England and British Lions.

24

The Game it is A-Changing

As I've said, rugby is very different now from the game I started playing seriously back in 1976. I have detailed in other stories how it has been transformed off the field but it has changed on the pitch as well -- and I'm not referring to the International Board decision to award five instead of four points for a try in 1992. The game at the top level has, since 1987, gradually become quicker with the advent of every new season.

Time was when a rugby player peaked at around twenty-eight or twenty-nine years old. In the 1990s top players are at their peak at around twenty-six years of age, and the way the game is going, that will soon be twenty-four or twenty-five. There are basically two reasons for this.

England's Test defeats against New Zealand in 1985 and Australia in 1988 convinced England manager Geoff Cooke that the English game had to be changed if we were to match the southern hemisphere teams. In Australia and New Zealand the grounds are invariably harder and that produces very fast rugby. To play at speed and keep the ball in hand requires considerable skill. In the late eighties the Aussies and Kiwis had developed into skilful speed merchants on the pitch. If we were to compete, England had to follow suit. Players had to be fitter, leaner and technically far better than their predecessors.

Geoff's quest to produce quicker, more skilful, rugby players was helped by the growth of the Courage Leagues. The league system offers clubs the opportunity to progress. To do this they have to compete and the higher up the league ladder they go, the more fierce the competition is. The days when a rugby player would turn up one night a week, run a few laps, do a few exercises, then spend the night in the bar exercising his right arm became, with the introduction of the league structure, a thing of the past.

At the top of the Courage League system, if you are not super-fit and technically adept, you do not play – it's as simple as that. If you did, the game would pass you by before a member of the opposition eventually took you out of the equation.

As the 1990s dawned, the archetypal top-class English rugby player was capable of speed as well as strength and possessed the handling ability of a master potter. In 1993 New Zealand toured the British Isles and beat everyone out of sight. I saw Scotland put to the sword by 51–15 at Murrayfield. The press waxed lyrical about the Kiwis, saying that when it came to international rugby they were in a different class from everyone else. On BBC TV's *Grandstand* I was asked for my opinion on how England would fare against New Zealand. I surprised my interviewer by saying that England would win by five clear points. I was wrong. At 15–9 they won by six.

The point I am making is that the media were slow to catch on to how much English rugby at the very top had changed in seven years. On their day England are now capable of beating anyone in the world. Our style, the pace at which we play the game and the way we move the ball are totally different. The two 'S's, speed and skill, have been paramount in the revolution. The Kiwis may have been able to come over and beat Scotland by a record margin in 1993 but at the time

I knew England's style and game had developed in such a way that it was out of the question that the Kiwis would walk over them.

As the game has got quicker and players' training geared towards them peaking on a Saturday, rugby has become more of a young man's game. It's sad but I think we have seen the last of the Wade Dooleys, Jeff Probyns and Paul Rendalls of this world.

Wade played his international rugby while at Preston Grasshoppers, a super club but not by any stretch of the imagination glamorous. When Wade was an England international, Preston Grasshoppers played in Courage League Five North. Wade was an enigma. He played only twelve or so matches a season. Don't get me wrong, he ran out on to the park for a total of perhaps thirty-three or thirty-four but in only twelve did he *really* play. He kept himself back for England internationals and the games in which the selectors were running the rule over him. He had this extraordinary ability to produce a wonderful performance when the occasion demanded. So not firing on all cylinders week in, week out and not having to face the very best opposition every Saturday enabled him to continue his international career into his late thirties.

There was a time when a prop would not come into his own until he was thirty-four; now a top-class prop is lucky to be still playing at thirty. Time catches up with us all and there's no use pretending otherwise. A player knows when it's time to hang up his boots. As Jack Rowell used to say on the subject of players getting older and trying to pretend they were as fit as they were at twenty-four: 'You can go on diets, you can visit saunas, you can have a hair transplant and buy youthful trendy clothes, but you'll never fool a flight of stairs.'

The sheer number of games in which top players are asked to take part nowadays also takes its toll. Time was when a club's fixture list would provide any number of easy friendly games in a season. Not now. The establishment of the league system ensures that you meet top-class opposition every week. If you are also called upon to play in the Five Nations, there simply is no respite. Like the leading cricketers, who seem to spend most of their year playing for their country rather than their counties, rugby players are playing more international rugby than ever before. Look back to when Bill Beaumont captained England in the early eighties: then a top international would reach twenty caps in six to seven years. In the nineties you can win twenty caps in eighteen months.

These days you don't see as many on-the-field punch-ups, or 'physical debates' as I call them. It's not that players are any less aggressive than their forebears – if anything they are stronger and more aggressive now than ever before. The reason for the lack of punch-ups is, again, speed. The game is too quick, it flows and it moves at a terrific pace. Players are not standing toe to toe eyeballing one another for minutes on end.

As I once said when squaring up to the Swansea, Cardiff and Wales powerhouse Dai Young, 'If you carry on niggling me, son, you're going to live up to your name.'

Another reason for the lack of physical debate is that rugby has emerged as a family game. As one who works in the media, I have seen posters of Bath's Ben Clarke and Harlequins' Will Carling in magazines aimed at the teenage-girl market. Can you ever imagine Fran Cotton, or even Tony Neary, as pin-ups for pubescent girls in the 1970s?

Parents bring their children, girls as well as boys, along to games. As a parent myself, I'm mindful that the very last thing to which you want to expose children is violence and uncontrollable aggression. Rugby is an aggressive and physical game, yes; but it is a controlled aggression, where reason rather than emotion is in the driving seat of the mind.

Some were slow to catch on to the fact that more and more families were spending Saturday afternoons at rugby matches.

One day in 1993 the commercial manager of a London-based Courage League One side rang me. He told me the club had just paid £4,000 to a market-research company to conduct a survey into the sort of people who are now attending rugby matches. The idea was that his club could target its commercial side more effectively and also provide facilities more in keeping with the demands of its supporters.

'Don't tell me,' I said, interrupting his flow. 'Whereas the crowd at a rugby match was once predominantly middle-class and male, we now have a lot of families. Parents bring girls as well as boys; and happily there are an increasing number of, and I use this term for want of a better one, "working-class" people attending rugby these days.'

'You've had research carried out at Bath as well, have you?' my fellow commercial manager asked.

'No,' I said. 'I just look around at the composition of the crowd at every home game.'

At Bath we fully recognise our obligation to our supporters and try to provide facilities in keeping with their requirements. One Sunday morning I was at the Rec chatting to a member of our ground committee, Rob Rowland. I remarked on the fact that more and more females were attending home games.

'Noticed that,' said Rob. 'We must build more female crappers around the ground.'

The point could have been made more delicately, I agree, but Rob was absolutely correct in his observation. What's more, it didn't cost Bath £4,000 to have it pointed out to them.

The pressure on international players these days is phenomenal. Terrestrial and Sky Television, radio and world press ensure saturation coverage for every international. With BBC TV's *Rugby Special* and SkySport analysing every move and kick the following day, it is little wonder that players sometimes feel apprehensive about trying something out of the ordinary in case it doesn't come off. The days when an England international like Dickie Jeeps could sit down to read the *Sunday Telegraph* and say to his wife, 'Look, darling, there's a piece here about yesterday's game,' are long passed.

Pressure affects players in different ways. Once changed, I used to sit quietly in the dressing room and psych myself up for the game ahead, whereas Rob Andrew would chatter away about anything that came into his head and crack witticisms.

'You know what I don't understand?' Rob once asked Brian Moore as they were changing.

'No. What?' asked Brian, thinking that Rob was about to make a point about the game plan that day.

'Latin!' said Rob.

Orrell's Dewi Morris used to be physically sick. Twenty minutes before the teams were due to leave the dressing room, without fail Dewi would take himself off into one of the loos for a technicolour yawn.

'Dewi? You really must stop watching *Surprise, Surprise!*' I'd shout after him.

Literally minutes before we were due out on the field, Nigel Redman would also pay a visit to the loo, but for him it was a proper sit-down job. In 1988, as the England team left the dressing room to play Fiji in Suva, Nigel 'Ollie' Redman was missing. I was instructed to go back and bring him out.

'C'mon Ollie. We're going out!' I shouted, popping my head around the door of the shower and loo area of the dressing room.

'I can't,' said Nigel in a somewhat pained voice. 'There's no paper.'

Looking around the room, I couldn't see paper of any description, never mind toilet paper. Mindful that we were now due out on the pitch, I grabbed a towel and threw it over the cubicle door. 'Use that!' I said to Nigel as I turned to join the team, who were taking the field.

The aftermath of it all was that the England selectors were

furious with Nigel and dropped him after that game. It would be two years before Nigel would play again for England and he still blames me for that time out of the England side. But how was I to know it was Will Carling's towel?

25

Rugby With Attitude

H TV SPORT once interviewed me about Bath's golden
decade between 1984 and 1994. 'It has been ten years of
wine, women and song,' said HTV sports presenter Roger
Malone as he started the interview.

'Well, I can't remember us doing much singing,' I replied.

It was unusual for me to be drawn into commenting on
Bath's success because, having had so much experience as a
player, you know better than to blow your own trumpet.
The next game might be a heavy defeat. You never know,
the next game could also be your last, and one game one
day will be.

Having played top-class rugby for seventeen years with the
most successful club side in the world, I realise that the dividing
line between success and failure is often very fine. Suspensions
apart, I never spent a lengthy period out of the game with
injury. I was fortunate. An injury doesn't have to be serious to
affect a playing career – a niggling minor problem that refuses to
go away can be enough to prevent a player being 100 per cent
fit. As Jack Rowell used to say, 'If you're not 100 per cent fit,
then you can't give 100 per cent in a game. So you're out!'

Nottingham's Gary Rees first got into the England team for

the game against Australia in 1984. Unfortunately a persistent injury prevented him from being fully fit for selection for quite some time afterwards. In fact, it was to be two years before Gary next appeared for England, against Ireland in 1986. When Bath visited Beeston to play Nottingham during Gary's time out of the England team I had a pint with him after the match. 'This period out of the game is getting me down, Coochie,' he told me.

'I know,' I said, looking at his drawn features. 'It's affecting your appearance.'

'It's not my appearance that bothers me,' said Gary. 'It's my disappearance!'

He was right, of course. Prolonged spells out of the game affect not only your physical fitness but your mental fitness too. At Bath we paid particular attention not only to physical preparation, high levels of skill and technique, but also to mental fitness.

Many rugby clubs think the mental approach to a game is the stamping of studs and the 'psyching up' beforehand. At Bath the attitude is different. It never involved kicking holes in dressing-room doors or proving that Graham Dawe or I could count past eight. What it did centre on was every one of us being cool under pressure. Take Graham Dawe. For the hooker to come out of the cauldron of a very physical, aggressive scrum and suddenly switch his mind to the ice-cool clarity necessary for an accurate throw requires a special mental agility. Many was the time I saw Jonathan Callard bundled over and given a raking and booting only to be clear-headed and calm taking a penalty less than a minute later. For Victor Ubogu to make a flying tackle necessitates physical ability but it also calls for supreme confidence to instigate the bravest of tackles in the first place. At Bath Jack Rowell and his successor, Brian Ashton, placed great emphasis on all players developing the right mental attitude, one which was considered to be the 'Bath way'.

On one occasion Bristol visted the Rec for what turned out to be a very ill-tempered and aggressive Courage League 'derby'. Midway through the second half a scrum started to wheel. The referee didn't blow up and so we carried on going round and round. When the referee's whistle finally put a stop to it, we'd been going round in circles for so long that Graham Dawe and Bristol's Alan Sharp went off the field suffering from spiral blood.

Bristol's scrum-half Kyran Bracken was eventually fed from the scrum but his pass out wide was intercepted by our outside-half, Mike Catt. Mike hesitated for only a split-second but it was too long and he disappeared under a hail of Bristol shirts. Mike, however, was determined to cling on to the ball at all costs.

'Give us the 'king ball or I'll rip your 'king head off!' Bristol's Andy Blackmore screamed.

Mike hung on regardless.

'Didn't you hear? I said release it or you'll have your 'king head ripped off!'

'I'm thinking it over!' Mike shouted back.

Now that is what I call the right attitude!

The right attitude also encompassed our physical training. I often speak to rugby players from junior clubs who tell me that a lion's share of their training sessions involves them running endless laps around the pitch. Not only is this largely ineffective in that it makes every player 'one-paced', it also has an adverse effect on the mental fitness of players as they are usually bored out of their minds after two laps.

Yes, we Bath players did train together as a group but only for certain parts of the training session, such as the warm-ups or stamina-building exercises. The greater emphasis was placed on training geared to the needs of the individual. It takes more organisation and effort on the part of the coach to introduce several mini-sessions for groups of three or four players rather than one big training session for everyone but it is essential if he wants to get the very best out of his team.

As a forward my needs in training were totally different from those of wingers Dave Trick and Tony Swift, for example. Their requirements, in turn, were different from those of flankers Andy Robinson and Jon Hall. Likewise Andy and Jon would need more speed training than me or our locks, Nigel Redman and Martin Haag; and none of us would need as much flexibility in our hamstrings as full-back Jon Callard, whose position demanded a lot of accurate kicking.

Jonathan Callard is one of the best tactical kickers I have encountered. Many was the time he would receive the ball when we were under the cosh deep in our own half and relieve the pressure with a fifty- or sixty-yard kick into touch. As a forward I know only too well that there is nothing more deflating than, having fought tooth and nail to progress deep into your opponents' half, suddenly to see a full-back of Jonathan's calibre kick into touch and send you back where you started from.

'It's all down to attitude and timing,' Jon told me when I asked him about tactical kicking as we travelled on the coach to an away game.

'At what point do you decide to actually kick it?' I asked.

'When I see someone like Leicester's Dean Richards or Orrell's Paul Manley getting within three yards of me,' he said.

As someone who was not noted for his ability to jink and side-step, I fully understood Jonathan's approach. Not being one of the game's speed kings, whenever he kicked the ball to within twenty yards of where I was on the pitch, I used to wind him up by giving him a rollicking. 'Why didn't you pass?' I'd scream. 'I was wide open!'

The right attitude plays a crucial part in any success, so it goes without saying that a negative attitude can have the opposite effect. At no time did I see this more clearly demonstrated than in Singapore Airport, of all places.

In 1988 I was a member of the England touring party which arrived in Singapore Airport Transit Lounge to board a flight to Brisbane. By coincidence the Welsh team were also there, waiting for their connecting flight out to Christchurch, New Zealand. The contrast between the two sides was amazing.

Even though the England party were preparing for an Aussie winter, the weather that awaited us in Brisbane was sunny with a temperature of around 68 degrees. In Singapore Airport all the England players changed into clothes suitable for the climate, tracksuit bottoms or chinos and polo shirts or T-shirts. The Welsh boys, on the other hand, stood around holding hooded all-weather tops and bench coats as they viewed the information board that told them the weather in Christchurch was wet and a maximum of 46 degrees.

Nigel Redman and I sat chatting with various Welsh lads and it was obvious they were not relishing the trip. Whereas the England players could look forward to the Australian version of winter sunshine offering surfing and golden beaches, the Welsh knew that what awaited them was ankle-deep mud and a series of tough games in which every opponent would want to put them to the sword. Even the normally irrepressible Jonathan Davies and John Devereux looked pensive and glum at the thought of Invercargill and its icy winds, seagulls and sheep.

As a player who cut his teeth on games against Welsh club sides and more often than not spent the return journey to England counting what I had left of those teeth, hoping the coach's suspension would be good enough to cushion my bruises from further aggravation on the bumps of the Severn Bridge, you might think I had no sympathy at all for the plight of those Welsh lads. You would be absolutely right!

In fact, in Bath we have a little ritual we perform every time we hear of a Welsh side going down to a heavy defeat.

We wear hair shirts, drink cod-liver oil and whack our fingers with a lump hammer — anything to stop us laughing.

In my salad days as a player I took more than my fair share of batterings from Welsh sides as they handed out one good hiding after another to those Bath teams of the late seventies. Not once, however, did I gripe or complain. So the sight of the Welsh team boarding that plane in Singapore, all with faces that would make Clement Freud look like the laughing clown outside Blackpool Funhouse, gave me a sadistic pleasure.

'They're going out to lose,' I said to Nigel Redman as we watched them depart. 'Their mental attitude is all wrong.'

Sadly for Wales it was a prophetic observation. They had a terrible time of it and lost the two Tests against the All Blacks by 52–3 and 54–9. I have a love-hate relationship with the Welsh and they with me but I took no pleasure in hearing of the emphatic defeats they suffered. After all, while many of those players were my adversaries on the pitch, off the field we were, and still are, the best of friends.

Following the two respective tours I bumped into Ieuan Evans at a sporting dinner in Newport and mentioned that I thought the Welsh team had been ill prepared mentally for the tour of New Zealand that had ended in disaster.

'You're absolutely right, Coochie,' Ieuan admitted. 'The only difference between us and the Titanic was the Titanic had entertainment!'

26

Perchance to Dream

I WAS always one of those players who had little trouble sleeping before a big game. In fact, it was after an important match that I had difficulty in winding down and relaxing. Even with the help of a few beers, when it came to bed, I found I had hyped and pumped myself up so much before and during the game itself that I was too keyed up for sleep, even seven or eight hours later.

Coaches are keen on players getting a good night's rest before a match. For an evening game, if possible, Jack Rowell used to like everyone to catch a couple of hours' sleep in the afternoon. Usually there is no problem with this, as heavy training schedules leave your body ready for rest at regular intervals.

The strangest incident of a player not being able to sleep at night concerned our scrum-half at Bath, Richard Hill. It occurred in 1992, and to this day Richard cannot say why he was able to get only fitful bouts of sleep for nights on end. Fortunately the problem eventually righted itself, as mysteriously as it had arisen.

The insomnia lasted for a fortnight or so and, while this does not seem that long, when you are snatching only two or three hours' sleep per night it quickly begins to have an adverse effect on your body. In the upper echelons of the Courage League players must gear their fitness and diet so that they peak on a Saturday. Richard was worried that his lack of sleep would cause a dip in his form.

To Richard's annoyance every night was the same. Unable to settle, he'd shift and shuffle in bed, irritated by imaginary itches. If it wasn't itching, then it was his pillows that would not lie right. After a week of it he even tried sleeping alone in the spare bedroom, but to no avail. As so often, the insomnia caused anxiety. Richard would lie awake, glance at the clock, see it was 3 or 4 a.m. and curse himself for not being able to sleep, knowing he was going to feel terrible in the morning.

The odd thing about Richard's condition was that, when he did fall asleep, he always dreamed about cricket. To some extent this is understandable as he is a very good cricketer, of minor counties standard, and at the time the new cricket season was only a matter of weeks away. After ten days of nightly purgatory, he looked a physical wreck and took up the matter with our club doctor.

'What's he given you?' I asked on bumping into Richard in the club car park as he was leaving the ground.

'Tablets, what else? The doc says they'll help me sleep.' Richard took the bottle of pills from his pocket to show me.

'And what did he have to say about you dreaming about cricket all the time?' I asked, genuinely concerned.

'He said I must be spending to much time thinking about the cricket season and, if I spent more of my conscious hours thinking about other things, the cricket thing would go away.'

'Well, that's what you're going to have to do from now on, then,' I said. 'Don't think about cricket at all today and tonight you won't dream about it.'

'Typical!' Richard said, shaking his head and tutting as he got into his car. 'Just my bloody luck.'

'How d'you mean?'

'Every night for the past week I've dreamed about being out in the field. Tonight it was my turn to bat!'

The only time pin-pointed by coaches as a period when players might have problems getting the required amount of sleep is when they have just got married.

Ann and I were married in 1989, not long before Bath played in the Pilkington Cup final against Leicester. More often than not on Sunday mornings the Bath players would pop into the ground to do a little light running to loosen tight limbs and to have any knocks and bruises from Saturday's game seen to by the physio. Our Sunday ritual was that Ann would drop me off at the ground, visit a friend who lived nearby for coffee and an hour later collect me from the club car park to drive us to a local restaurant or pub for Sunday lunch.

Jack Rowell was familiar with this routine. On the Sunday before the final he kept an eye out for Ann's arrival and went out to speak to her as she pulled into the car park.

After a few social niceties Jack came straight to the point. 'You and Gareth have just been married,' he said, 'and it goes without saying that the first few weeks of marriage tend to be . . . how can I put it, Ann? The time when a man and wife are most passionate?'

Ann nodded to indicate that she followed his drift.

'Normally when a player gets married, it would have nothing at all to do with me. But we have the Pilkington Cup final coming up this Saturday. The whole club – the whole city, in fact – is looking for Gareth to be at his best – mentally, playing-wise and physically. Now, because you two have only just been married and because of this important match, I want you to have these.' He took a bottle from his pocket and showed it to Ann. 'They're sleeping tablets,' said Jack. 'Normally I wouldn't inter- fere with matrimonial matters but these are exceptional circumstances. We need Gareth in peak physical shape next week.'

Ann took the bottle, which contained about ten tablets.

'To be taken five minutes before bedtime,' said Jack. 'That way they'll ensure no passion play and sound sleep right through to the next morning.'

Ann nodded and popped the bottle into her handbag. 'And how many does Gareth have to take each night?' she asked.

Jack stared at her with a surprised look on his face. 'They're not for Gareth,' he said incredulously. 'They're for you!'

27

The Cheeky Watch

IT WAS a freezing cold, dark night at Lambridge. A biting wind added to the chill factor and made ball-handling difficult. After half an hour my fingers felt like lobster's claws and had a similar speed of movement. The icy mud squelched ankle-high about our boots as the first-XV squad were put through their paces by Jack Rowell. Every time we stopped for further instruction, sweat condensation rose from our backs as if we were horses at the end of the Grand National.

It's a strange thing but you can always tell those not used to any form of training. At any club, at any level, they will turn up for their first session in pristine tracksuit and boots polished like glass. Not so those who regularly put themselves through the twice-weekly training routine. Bath players are no different from any others when it comes to training kit. They look as if they have all snatched whatever they could from a church jumble sale.

Layering clothes became somewhat fashionable in the early 1990s. In rugby it has always been standard wear for training. First an old T-shirt. On top of that a rugby shirt that has seen better days. Then a thick cotton sweatshirt and a rainproof top. Leg wear is more colourful than anything Zandra Rhodes could create. Players always have more socks than tracksuit bottoms, so socks and shorts are always worn over the tracksuit so that the trousers need not be washed at the end of every session. Socks and shorts are easy to wash and dry, not so tracksuit bottoms. And what a harlequin selection of socks there are on display. Socks, as everyone knows, have a habit of going missing singly, which is why few players are ever seen wearing a pair for training that are the same colour, never mind match.

The other prerequisite of the winter-night training session is the woollen bobble hat. With 40 per cent of body heat lost through the head, most elect to wear one as it aids what we call 'getting a good sweat on'. You'd think with all this clothing you'd sweat like a bull during winter training but, with the night air being so cold, the body does not have to work as hard as it does in the summer to cool you down. Wear only a thin T-shirt and a pair of shorts for a pre-season training session in July, however, and the perspiration runs from your body in rivulets.

Winter training is a dirty, muddy affair, not to say unwelcome. After a hard day's work you'd rather draw the curtains, put your feet up in front of a crackling fire and watch TV. When you get in from work the thought of having to slosh about for two hours on a pitch that resembles Passchendaele in driving sleet tests even the most dedicated of players.

So winter training is not where you'd expect to see anyone wearing good sportswear, and certainly not an expensive Rolex watch.

There'd been some playful banter this particular January night in 1991. The news of the day had carried the story that, as part of their updating process, the waxwork dummy of me had been removed from display in Madame Tussaud's.

'They're going to melt it down and turn it into the Nolans.' quipped Richard Hill.

'What did the wife get you for Christmas?' Stuart Barnes asked Jerry Guscott.

'Well, believe it or not, one of the things she bought me was a book,' said Jerry.

'I read a book once,' interrupted Graham Dawe. 'It were green.'

Jerry Guscott was smirking to himself, so Stuart asked him what he was so pleased about.

'This book,' said Jerry. 'It's *The Illustrated Joys of Love-Making*.'

'You'll be borrowing your daughter's crayons to colour it in, then,' said Stuart.

The players were in fine fettle but for some weeks Jack Rowell had been distant and more offhand than usual with everyone, his face more inscrutable than ever. I always got on well with Jack. I had and still have the greatest respect for him as a man and a coach. Quite simply I have not come across a better coach. If he can be judged by the silverware he has won, then Jack is far out in a class of his own. For some reason, though, he had had a particular downer on me for a fortnight or so. I just couldn't seem to do anything right for him, in training or in games.

Jack had the first-XV squad doing timed shuttle runs. Damian Cronin had turned up for training even though he was injured and Jack had enlisted him to help out. He handed Damian his watch and warned him to look after it. We set about doing our shuttle runs, watched by Jack and timed by Damian, who noted each player's individual running time on a clipboard.

The first round of shuttle runs over, Jack checked everybody's times. 'You're slower than steam off a dog turd, Coochie,' he said to me sternly.

'I wouldn't say Jack's being disagreeable tonight,' Phil de Glanville said to me, 'but he's being one of those things you find at the top of women's legs.'

I nodded. Graham Dawe looked at Phil, somewhat puzzled. 'Jack's being a suspender belt?'

The night was very frosty and the shuttle runs were conducted in an equally frosty way. When they ended, I made my way over to Damian.

'Damian, give me Jack's watch,' I said. 'Just going to have a bit of fun, see if I can put a smile on his face.'

Damian handed over the watch and my eyes popped. It was a top-of-the-range Rolex. I'd have been a nervous wreck wearing it to a formal dinner, never mind bringing it to training.

I caught up with the rest of the players on their way to the dressing room. We were soon joined by Jack.

'Right, you lot, where is it?' asked Jack. It was obvious from his tone that he was in a no-nonsense mood. 'Come on, hand it over. Which one of you buggers took my watch?'

I stepped forward and pulled down my shorts and tracksuit bottoms to reveal that I was wearing nothing underneath.

'I cannot tell a lie,' I said coyly, smiling and fluttering my eyes. 'T'was I!'

I leaned forward, stretched out my hands before me and stopped clenching my buttocks together to allow the Rolex to drop from between the cheeks of my bottom on to the frozen pitch.

Jack screamed in horror.

Nigel Redman, Graham Dawe, Andy Robinson, Jon Hall – in fact all of the first-XV squad – convulsed with laughter.

Jack ran to a nearby hedge and returned with a stick. Gingerly he picked up the Rolex with the end of the stick and hurriedly took it over to the tap on the outside of the changing rooms which we used to wash the mud from our boots.

He was furious as he turned the tap full-flow on his valuable watch. 'I've never known such cheek!' he said, po-faced.

'Well, they are a bountiful pair, that's for sure!' I called out on my way into the changing rooms. Whether or not the water had an adverse effect on that super Rolex watch, I don't know. We players never saw it again.

28

Scrum Fun

A T CARDIFF Arms Park or Murrayfield on a bitterly cold January afternoon, when an icy wind cuts through the thickest coat like a hot knife through butter, it's cosy and warm in a scrum.

We forwards aren't as daft as we look. We tell the backs that it is sheer bloody murder in a scrum just in case they should ever want to join us. That is why, in the Five Nations or Courage Leagues, you'll see full-backs like Rob Andrew, Jonathan Callard and Paul Hull shivering with the cuffs of their shirtsleeves pulled down over their hands in an attempt to keep warm.

Forwards like me are not built to run around and keep warm, so when we feel the cold, it's time to scrum down. In the England team the forwards refer to the backs as the 'girls', whereas the forwards are known by the backs simply as the forwards. Backs may feel the cold, but they're not stupid.

In 1979 Bath's learning curve under Jack Rowell continued with another visit to the Park, the home of Pontypool and that formidable front row of Graham Price, Bobby Windsor and Charlie Faulkner. They may well have seen better days together but they could still be redoubtable opponents, especially to a young rookie like me. I had played against them on four previous occasions, so I was becoming familiar with them and they with me, as became apparent during the first scrum.

It was a filthy day and we were playing amid a constant freezing drizzle. Clouds of vapoured sweat rose from our backs as we set to. There was the sound of collarbone grinding on collarbone and I remember gouging my boot deep into the mud to try to find some firm earth in which to get an anchorage.

As we waited for the ball to be fed in, I felt a set of teeth clip on to my right earlobe, then suddenly let go. 'Behave yourself, son, and nothing will happen to this ear of yours,' Bobby Windsor said, and promptly gripped my ear again with his teeth.

It was then that I felt a hand gently slap my face. 'Just lining you up for a punch, should you start any of your shenanigans, Coochie, son,' I heard Graham Price's voice, to my left, warn.

'And if by chance you were thinking of starting anything today, son,' – a hand, to this day I don't know whose, took a firm hold of my testicles – 'then think on. It would be a tragedy for someone as young as you to have something happen to these.' The hand gave my testicles a gentle squeeze. I shifted uncomfortably but carefully.

Teeth clenching my ear, my face being lined up for a punch and a hand gripping my testicles was bad enough, but as the *pièce de résistance*, when the ball came into the scrum, Charlie Faulkner put two fingers up my nostrils! Believe it or not, we nearly won that one against the head.

Graham, Bobby and Charlie, frightening as they were on the pitch, always made time afterwards to offer me the benefit of their experience. It was Charlie who advised me to put my feet further back when in a scrum. 'You'll feel more comfortable that way, son.'

Bobby told me where to place my arms to lessen the chance of having them broken and always to try to look up and keep the back straight. This way, Bobby told me, I would get maximum driving force and it would reduce the risk of injury to myself and prevent the scrum from collapsing. It was excellent advice for a young forward like me and as the years passed I marvelled at how good it was of Graham, Bobby and Charlie to pass on the fruits of their considerable experience. Without doubt they were very physical to play against but they always kept within the spirit of the game. Looking back, I recognise they were not only great rugby players but great sportsmen, in every sense of the word. As I became one of the game's experienced players, I was ever mindful to offer tips and help to any young player willing to listen.

When forwards form a scrum, if you win possession of the ball when it has been fed in by the opposition, it is called winning the ball against the head. In the 1991–2 Pilkington Cup final against Harlequins, Graham Dawe, Victor Ubogu and I twice claimed we had won the ball against the head when in fact it had been accidentally kicked forward by Harlequins prop Andy Mullins.

As we celebrated our victory, by 15–12, in the dressing room, captain Andy Robinson complimented us on winning scrums against the head. Fuelled by best bitter, Graham, Victor and I told him, 'That's what comes of having good forwards in the team.' As Andy concluded his lavish praise, scrum-half Richard Hill wandered over.

'That's a terrible nervous twitch Andy Mullins has in his right knee,' he said knowingly.

Never have three forwards suddenly gone so very sheepish and quiet.

It is the job of the scrum-half to put the ball into the scrum along the axis midway between the two opposing front rows. In top-flight rugby the scrum-half and hooker know through hours of practice when the ball should be fed. An ill-timed ball into the scrum against a Courage League side generally resulted in your opponents disrupting the strike, if not winning it, whereas a quick, clean put-in ensured possession nearly every time, even when we were under pressure.

England, like Bath, had a variety of signals and these would change from time to time so that the opposition would not be aware of them. In essence they were very simple signals, something like a tap, but they needed to be short and sharp to be undetectable. There was a time with England in the late eighties, however, when the various signals between scrum-half and hooker got very involved, to the point of being plain silly.

When we played the USA at the Concord Oval in Sydney during the 1987 World Cup, the taps became ridiculously complicated. Midway through the first half scrum-half Richard Hill was faffing about with the ball at the put-in. I was aware of a number of taps on Graham Dawe's shoulder. They were so numerous and so quick you'd have thought it was Morse code. 'What did it say?' I asked, knowing a signal had been made.

'We go on ahead with the girl. The sheriff's going to try to head them off at the gulch,' said Graham.

That particular scrum eventually collapsed, but only because we were all incapable with laughter.

During England's 1988 tour of Australia we encountered what RFU officials referred to as 'certain referees who implemented different standards to those expected'. Or, to the rest of us, cheating bastards.

We were involved in a tight struggle with a South Australia XV at the Barton Oval in Adelaide when, for the umpteenth time, the opposing scrum-half, Mick Catchpole, fed the ball crooked into the scrum. At no time had this crooked put-in ever been to our advantage, and not once did referee Younger blow up for the infringement.

Twenty minutes into the second half I had had enough of it. 'When they have the put-in,' I complained, pointing to the opposition, 'that ball hasn't once come in straight!'

'That last put-in was straight as a die,' referee Younger said defensively.

'Bollocks!' I said, getting all fired up. 'That ball went in between their second row and back row!'

'That's as maybe,' said Younger, 'but it went in straight.'

Characters – Famous and Unsung

'People are always quick to admit to a player's ability once he has made it to the top.'

Ken Bolam, composer and musician.

'At Bath we won many a game in the last minute. We had so many great escapes, I half expected to look across to the replacement bench and see Steve McQueen.'

Ben Clarke, Bath, England and British Lions.

29

Dirty Bertie

C LUB TOUR itineraries, like the takeaway menu for the
local Indian restaurant and guarantees for appliances that
have gone wrong, can never be found when you want them.

I don't know why this is. All I know is, it is so. The Bath
or England secretary would send me a tour itinerary weeks
before departure. It would detail dates and times of fixtures,
the addresses, telephone and fax numbers of the hotels where
we were staying, flight departure times, assembly points – in
fact everything you needed to know. The night before we set
off I'd be taking the house apart trying to find it.

'I remember thinking, I'll put this away somewhere safe so
I don't lose it,' I'd say to Ann.

'So safe you can't find it,' she'd reply.

If she said that once she must have said it a dozen
times.

Eventually I'd ring Richard Hill to find out where we were
meeting and when. I'd always end up photocopying his itinerary
at the first hotel we came to. When the time comes for Ann and
me to move house, I bet I'll find the itineraries for getting on
for twenty tours.

It's odd, because in every other way I consider myself to be exceptionally well organised and up to speed. This is touring for you. It changes a person. It's a bit like those people who behave primly and properly at home in front of the neighbours but frolic naked in a drunken stupor in front of a beach of strangers when on holiday. Travel does something to people. It changes them into another animal, albeit temporarily. For two weeks or however long we are away, we cast aside self and become another person. Set foot back in our homes and Mr Hyde reverts to Dr Jekyll as the normal self returns to the body. I've seen it happen to dozens and dozens of players. The most acute case was Bert Meddick.

I liked Bert Meddick a lot. He was a prop with Bath in the late seventies and a good one at that. In order to be a prop you have to be a little crazy. It's a prerequisite of the job in much the same way as it is for soccer goalkeepers and the cliff-divers of Acapulco. So Bert was a little crazy at times. On tour, however, he was practically demented.

Before the rugby revolution of the mid-eighties and its emphasis on speedy, skilful rugby, you often found two veteran props in every rugby team. There seemed to be an unwritten rule that no prop could retire until he was forty-five. Consequently clubs had to accommodate props coming through the ranks as best they could. That is why in the second or third XVs of junior clubs in the seventies you'd often find six or seven props filling all manner of positions, including fly-half and scrum-half. Before the revolution props emerged at around twenty-eight years of age. What a prop did before that, like the workings of the human appendix, remains a mystery.

On away trips within these shores Bert Meddick was excellent company. Winger Dave Trick and I would sit and natter away with him about all the great mysteries of life — not mysteries such as UFOs or the *Marie Celeste* but those that touch on our everyday lives.

The team coach would be passing through the countryside

when Bert would turn to Dave and me. 'Here's one for you. Ever been out with the family and you see a field like that,' he would say, pointing to a beautiful, sloping meadow. 'You think, that will be ideal for a picnic. But come the picnic and sitting in the field, it always turns out to be bumpy, full of thistles and cow shit and impossible to sit and relax in.'

Dave and I would nod our heads in recognition.

'How come a chair leg scraping on the floor can sound like a fart but no one ever confuses a fart with a chair leg scraping on the floor?'

'Listen to Bert,' I'd say, nudging Dave in the ribs. 'This is wisdom!'

'Too true, it is,' Bert would say and continue to spout forth his mysteries.

'At the beginning of *Star Trek* they say that Captain Kirk and the crew of the *Starship Enterprise* boldly go where no man has gone before. If that's the case, how come wherever Kirk and his crew went, they always met someone?'

And so Bert would continue. Question after question; mystery after mystery.

'Why, in films, when there is a sword fight, do they always end up fighting on the top of a large table? Why does a giant candlestick always get sliced in half? When the bad guy drops his sword, why does the good guy always allow him pick it up again? When the good guy drops his sword – and he always does – why does the bad guy always continue to thrust and slash at the good guy? Why does the good guy always pick up the giant candlestick to defend himself? Why not the sword again?'

When Dave or I asked for explanations, Bert would always say the same thing. 'If I told the truth, you'd never believe me.'

In the late seventies Bath were dipping their toe into touring. The first tentative tours were being undertaken under the guidance of Jack Rowell. We didn't travel far – France was the farthest to start with — but it was distance enough for a teenager like me. I was of the opinion that only 'proper' rugby players toured and I thought I'd really arrived on the rugby scene simply because I was touring.

In 1977, when we were off on tour to France, to keep costs down we took an overnight ferry from Portsmouth to Cherbourg from where our coach would take us on to games in Valognes, Caen and Lisieux. If you know your geography of France you will realise that we did not venture far from the northern coastline. It mattered not one jot to me, however. To me, the lad who had been overjoyed to go on his first away trip with Old Redcliffians to Torquay, Normandy seemed like the other side of the world.

Bath had embarked upon a similar short tour the year before and had stopped off at a lovely café called Le Poulet in Cherbourg on arriving in France and also on the return leg. It was decided that on disembarking from the ferry we should visit Le Poulet en masse for breakfast.

The night before had seen a heavy crossing, not sea-wise but drinking-wise. I distinctly recall Jim Waterman staring into my half-open eyes as we took a morning consti-tutional around the deck before docking. 'You should donate blood when we dock,' he said. 'They'd get a pint out of each eye.'

The players gathered by the gangway as we docked and Roger Spurrell, who was counting heads, announced we were one short. It was quickly established that our prop, Bert Meddick, was the missing party.

As I have said, people change once they are away from their normal environment. Travel and distant places turn shrew-like creatures into daredevils and strait-laced souls into lusting exhibitionists. As we were to discover, Bert Meddick, a bright, humorous but somewhat staid guy who liked a drink, but never to excess, had turned into a cross between Oliver

Reed, Hurricane Higgins and Bernard Manning before the ferry had passed the Isle of Wight.

Roger, anxious that he be found quickly, dispatched the rest of the players in pairs to look for Bert. Jim and I were given the second floor of the ferry to comb. On passing the children's play room, we decided to investigate the screams and shrieks of laughter that were emanating from within.

We quietly opened the door and recognised the voice immediately. It was Bert.

A group of about ten children aged from six to nine were sitting on the floor in front of the playroom's Punch and Judy stall. Bert was operating Mr and Mrs Punch from behind the curtain and Jim and I stood, gobsmacked, as his slurred voice, obviously very much the worse for alcohol, sang as Mr Punch to Mrs Punch:

> There was a young girl from Tottenham
> Her manners? She'd simply forgotten 'em
> During tea at the vicar's
> She took off her knickers
> Because she was feeling too hot in 'em.

The children shrieked with delight. Bert then operated Mrs Punch in such a way that she bent over with her rear facing Mr Punch. He made the sound of a resounding fart.

'That's what I think of your song, Mr Punch,' said Bert in a passable Mrs Punch voice.

The children screamed with laughter and clapped their hands with glee. Jim and I made our way to the rear of the Punch and Judy stall and pulled Bert out. Drunk as a lord, he stood swaying before us with a silly grin on his face, a fag in the corner of his mouth and the puppets still on his hands.

As we had never known Bert smoke before, Jim took the cigarette from his lips while I removed the puppets from his hands. 'C'mon, Bert. We're docking in Cherbourg. It's time to go,' I said as we propelled him out of the room.

From his advanced condition it was obvious that Bert had been up all night drinking.

'I've still got half a bottle of brown in there,' he slurred, pointing back over his shoulder as Jim and I marched him out of the room and into the corridor.

Up on deck we passed an irate couple with a small girl. The parents, in their mid-twenties, were furiously complaining to one of the ferry's officers.

'Call that a children's entertainer? He told the kids his name was Uncle Farty Arse! What sort of children's entertainer is that?'

Jim and I hurriedly frogmarched the benignly smiling Bert past the fuming parents to the gangway and the waiting Jack Rowell and Roger Spurrell.

'Where on earth have you been?' Jack asked Bert.

Bert stared back with what now seemed to be a permanent silly grin.

'We found him asleep on one of the chairs in the lounge bar,' I cut in before Bert could say anything to incriminate himself.

'Well, help him get his gear together,' said Jack. 'We're breakfasting at Le Poulet in twenty minutes.'

Le Poulet stayed open till two in the morning and opened again for breakfast at five. The Gachasin family, who ran it, were friendly, warm and accommodating. Their house speciality was milk-simmered leg of lamb in a caper sauce with roasted pears. They told us that to be enjoyed at its best, it had to be accompanied by copious amounts of wine. Who were we to argue?

As we sat in groups of four and five around the circular tables draped with red and white gingham tablecloths, the smell of roasted coffee, freshly baked croissants and cinnamon toast wafting through from the kitchens literally made our mouths water.

I was at a table in a corner of the restaurant with Dave Trick, Charlie Ralston, Jim Waterman, Brian Jenkins and Bert Meddick, who by this time was looking decidedly unwell. He sat rigidly in silence as the rest of us chatted about the quality of the food.

'I've never tasted cinnamon toast as good as they make here,' I remarked.

'It's because they use fresh cinnamon and *brioches* instead of ordinary white bread,' said Charlie.

'*Brioches?*' asked Brian.

'Yeah, they're soft rolls they make from a very light yeast dough. They're a speciality of the Normandy region. We had them last year, didn't we Bert?'

Bert's face didn't move a muscle. He stared straight ahead into space. He had a worried look that I didn't like at all. His eyes were wide open and transfixed on some spot way beyond my right shoulder. His expression was one of concern and anxiety, as if he were awaiting some impending doom. He sat bolt upright and motionless with both hands palms down on the edge of the table. The conversation suddenly stopped as Dave, Charlie, Jim and Brian became aware of his condition.

Charlie Ralston, who was sitting on Bert's left, patted his hand to reassure him. 'Are you feeling all right, old man?' he asked, genuinely concerned.

Bert didn't respond. His facial expression didn't change one iota. He still sat there bolt upright, staring into space.

'Bert?' asked Charlie softly. 'You all right, mate?'

Nothing.

'Perhaps we should walk him round the block to get some fresh air,' Jim Waterman suggested.

'Yes. Fancy a walk with me and Jim?' asked Charlie.

Still no response.

'I'm no doctor,' I said, 'but he looks in a bad way to me. As if something is troubling him.'

Charlie nodded. 'Is that it? Is something bothering you? Did something happen on the ferry?'

Nothing.

'Bert? If it did, you can tell us,' Charlie persisted in soft tones. 'We're not only your team-mates, we're your friends.'

We all nodded. Still nothing.

'Listen, Bert,' Charlie continued. 'You've been drinking all night. Something is troubling you. Do you want to rid yourself of it?'

To the great relief of the five of us, Bert nodded his head slowly.

'Then go ahead. We're your friends,' said Charlie.

The corners of Bert's lips moved upwards ever so slightly as he offered us a pained and grateful smile.

Paaaaaaaawwwwwwwwwwwwwwwwwwaaaaarrrrrrrrrrrrrrrrrrppppp!

The loudest and longest fart I have ever heard ripped across the room.

Charlie Ralston shot back in his chair.

Dave, who was on the other side of Bert, jumped up but had nowhere to go as he was hemmed in a corner. Everyone in the restaurant, players, locals and staff, immediately stopped their conversations in mid-flow and turned to stare at our table in silent disbelief.

Bert, too, sat in silence. A glowing smile of satisfaction appeared on his face, then a look of pride. It was short-lived. Suddenly it was replaced by a look of total horror.

'Argggghhh, lemme out!' Dave Trick screamed before scrambling across the tabletop to escape his imprisonment in the corner. It was then that the vilest of smells wafted up from Bert. Our faces contorted and we all clutched our napkins to our noses. Dave was joined by two waitresses out on the pavement outside, all three taking in huge gulps of fresh air.

'I think I'm going to be sick,' said Charlie as he quickly rose from the table and headed for the Gents'.

My eyes started to water. I held the napkin tight against my mouth and nose.

'I've followed through,' simpered Bert.

'What?' I asked in a muffled voice from behind the napkin.

'I've followed through,' Bert repeated pathetically, on the point of tears.

I turned to the napkinned faces of Jim Waterman and Brian Jenkins. 'What does he mean, he's followed through?'

'He's bloody well shit himself, that's what he's done!' said Brian.

As members of the Gachasin family frantically busied themselves with opening windows and spraying air-fresheners, Bert slowly took to his feet. Sliding from the table, he walked like Groucho Marx in slow motion across the room. Legs bent, back sloping forward, backside protruding, he gingerly took one step after another as the entire restaurant looked on, and disappeared into the Gents'.

Ten minutes later a sheepish Bert returned as the rest of us started to tuck into our croissants.

'Haven't you cleaned up?' asked Dave Trick, angered as the foul smell returned to haunt us.

'Course I have,' said Bert defensively.

'Then what's that disgusting smell?' I asked.

'These!' replied Bert, holding up his underpants.

'Bloody hell! Get rid of those!' Charlie snapped, almost choking on a mouthful of croissant. 'And now!'

Bert again left the table and moments later returned.

'What on earth goes through your head when we go on

tour, Bert?' I asked.

'The same as goes through his arse,' said Charlie, shaking his head in disbelief.

By contrast the rest of the tour passed off incident-free. We won all three games and the Bath club officials decided to treat us to a meal in Le Poulet before we caught the ferry back to Portsmouth.

The trauma of the beginning of the tour had resulted in Bert maintaining rather a low profile for the remainder, more in keeping with his normal self, in fact. As Dave, Charlie, Jim, Brian, Bert and I sat back sipping coffee after the sumptuous leg of lamb and roast pears, Bert suddenly held up a finger in the air. 'Excuse me, there's something I've got to get.'

He left the table and went across to a radiator by the bar area. We watched in amazement as he reached behind it and fished around for a few moments. Suddenly his face lit up. 'Here they are!' he said, pleased as punch, and produced from behind the radiator his soiled underpants, now as stiff as cardboard.

We all sat open-mouthed, not believing what we were seeing. So shocked were we that not one of us protested when Bert returned and tapped the stiffened underpants on the table. 'I've got to take them home. It's the wife, you see. She counts the pairs of underpants I take on tour. If I returned minus a pair, she'd think I'd been up to no good with some other woman.'

A look of satisfaction crept across Bert's face and he lovingly prised open the foul underwear.

'It's a mystery to me why you didn't just bin them and tell her the truth,' said Charlie.

'If he told the truth, she'd never believe him!' chorused Dave Trick and I, as if on cue.

Bert stared at the underpants. 'How come,' he said reflectively, 'it's always when you're half-way through your business on the loo that you notice there's no toilet paper?'

'He knows he's almost home,' said Dave.

We all nodded.

30

Old Ken

ONE OF the advantages of being on the after-dinner circuit is that you get to meet well-known people from other sports. Occasionally you get to meet a true legend, as I have in the case of soccer genius George Best. Many people have a pre-conceived idea about what George is like as a person. Often it is completely inaccurate, based on newspaper reports that, to use a political term, are 'economical with the truth'. I have run into George on the after-dinner circuit a number of times now, and he comes across to me as a highly intelligent, warm, caring and sensitive person.

Speakers who try to rip off clubs and organisations by charging fees far in excess of their worth or give poor value in the way of a speech are short-lived on the circuit. Reputations are made quickly and soon the bookings peter out to nothing. George Best, like me, I'd like to think, always gives value for money with a speech that not only gives an insight into his career but provides plenty of laughs into the bargain. I don't think it is any exaggeration to say that George and I could be out doing a dinner every night of the week, fifty-two weeks a year, but for other commitments and a justifiable concern for our waistlines.

At one particular dinner George and I found ourselves chatting about films, in particular films with a sporting theme or which deal with a famous sporting person. We both agreed that we had seen only two such films that were really good. What's more, our choices were the same: Lindsay Anderson's 1963 version of David Storey's novel *This Sporting Life*, which uses Rugby League as a metaphor for the rat race, and Martin Scorsese's 1980 masterpiece of men and male values, *Raging Bull*, about the 1949–51 middleweight world champion Jake la Motta.

As George and I chatted, he mentioned the character called Dad, played by William Hartnell, in *This Sporting Life*. He is a supporter-cum-self-appointed scout who hangs around the City Rugby League club. George told me of a similar old guy he knew simply as Walter who lurked around Manchester United day in and day out in the sixties and had apparently done so for some forty years. Walter never got paid and no one knew how he got by. Like Dad in *This Sporting Life*, he simply worshipped all the players with schoolboy enthusiasm and would do anything to help them. George and I concluded that no matter what the sport, every club had a Dad or a Walter. And not only every club, as I pointed out to him; the England rugby team had one at Twickenham.

He was known as Old Ken. I have asked around but no one can recall ever knowing his surname. Ken was in his eighties when I came across him during my time with the England team in the 1980s. As far as I can establish, he had started hanging around Twickenham just after the Second World War. Originally he used to help out the groundsmen with the pitch and by making tea and running errands for them. Eventually Ken was given jobs around the ground, like sweeping corridors or the changing rooms after a game, anything and everything really. Players came and went but Ken remained as a 'gofer' for anybody who needed him.

He wasn't paid and I don't know how he supported himself, but somehow he did.

Of all the players Ken worshipped, without doubt far and away his favourite was big Fran Cotton, the Coventry and Sale forward. Fran's England career encompassed thirty-one appearances between 1971 and 1981 but, even when big Fran's England playing days were over, he still found himself visiting Twickenham for internationals, initially with the rugby press and latterly as the co-director of Cotton Traders, the company that supplies the official England strip and kit.

From Fran's very first appearance against Scotland in 1971 Ken took to him. In the ensuing years, whatever Fran wanted, Ken would be there to carry out his wish. Chips from down the road, a newspaper, chewing gum, a birthday card for a relative: whatever it was, Fran would simply call for Ken. He would give Ken the money and off the old boy would go, whistling to himself, proud at having attention from the great Fran Cotton.

As the years passed, Old Ken acquired a room for himself at Twickenham. I say room, but that is rather a grand title for it, for in truth it was no more than a narrow broom and mop cupboard, some six or seven feet deep, which led off the corridor along from the home-team dressing room. Nevertheless, over the years Ken made it 'his room'.

With hooks for the brushes, dustpans, buckets and a shovel on one side and shelving for cleaning materials on the other, there was no room to swing a cat. At the far end Ken had managed to introduce a chair, and on the shelf by the only plug point he found room for a kettle and tea-making paraphernalia. There was precious little space on the walls but what there was had been filled with press cuttings and photographs of Fran Cotton's games at Twickenham.

If any of the Twickenham groundstaff or officials needed Ken and could not find him jobbing about, they knew they would find him in his room — unless Fran Cotton was around, that is. Ken had only to hear that Fran had arrived and he was there at his beck and call. At the drop of a hat he'd be off on an errand. It really infuriated the Twickenham groundstaff and officials.

Time and time again a head would pop around the dressing-room door. 'Anyone seen old Ken?'

'He's gone out for Cotton,' someone would say.

'Seen Old Ken? We need him to put towels out in the officials' changing room.'

'He's gone to put a bet on for Fran Cotton.'

Every game was the same, year after year.

'Where the hell is Ken? He's not in his room. Don't tell me, he's gone on an errand for Cotton.'

The players would nod their heads.

In 1988 Old Ken passed away. Fran had heard about it and turned up to watch the England international against Ireland clutching a small brown-paper package. Being the nosy sort, I asked him what was in it.

'A personal tribute to Old Ken,' said Fran. 'I had it made up. It's for his door.'

After the game I was about to join my England team-mates to celebrate our 35–3 victory when I remembered Fran's tribute and decided to go back along the corridor to see what it was.

There on the door of Old Ken's room was a polished rosewood plaque on which was screwed a small brass plate. The inscription on the plate was short and simple:

OLD KEN

GONE . . . BUT NOT FOR COTTON

As part of the massive redevelopment of Twickenham, Old Ken's room was demolished. I just hope the powers that be have found a place somewhere for Fran's tribute to his faithful friend.

31

Jeff Probyn

JEFF PROBYN was an outstanding forward with Wasps, Askeans and, of course, England, for whom he made thirty-seven appearances. He retired from the international scene after playing in England's 17–3 defeat in Dublin against Ireland in 1993. It could and should have been a more fitting finale for a player who literally shed blood, sweat and tears for his country and never once complained when he was on the receiving end of a physical battering.

Jeff was, if anything, an all-out player whose indomitable spirit carried him through when things weren't going his way on the pitch. Without a doubt Ireland deserved to win that 1993 encounter. That said, on the day England were bitterly disappointing.

Jeff holds the Wasps record for most appearances as a forward in the Courage Leagues with sixty-four. It was he, along with Rob Andrew, Chris Oti, Steve Bates and Mark Bailey, who formed the cornerstone of the Wasps side which emerged as one of the major forces in league rugby since its inception in 1987–8.

To me Jeff is something of an enigma for, while one side of him is smack-bang up to date with modern technology and thinking, another part is curiously out of step with contemporary mores and values. As one would expect of someone as forthright in thought and opinion as Jeff, such a combination of attitudes has occasionally landed him in hot water.

Supporters like to think of their team as being the best of friends, exemplifying a cavalier, 'all for one and one for all' attitude, and this is true in many cases. But by the law of averages, when fifteen and more players are brought together by one common denominator, the coach/manager, you will find that often there will be some who do not get on. You must play as a team, however, and if you find yourself alongside a player to whom you don't particularly warm, then the very least you can do for your coach, team and supporters is to put personal differences to the back of your mind and respect that man as a player. You respect his ability, what he does for your team and qualities such as his motivation, bravery and application. In time you hope that you will get to understand him better and perhaps to like him.

Just think of your own working environment. Can you honestly say that you are the best of friends with everyone there? More to the point, when backs are against the wall, could you in all honesty say that you would put your head on the block and risk life and limb for all of them in order to fight your way out of a corner? You have to in top-class rugby, even when you may have a team-mate or two who could give irritability lessons to Saddam Hussein.

The coach brings the players together and hopes that everyone will mix well. The coach is out there alone. He can't afford to form close friendships with players, no matter how long they have been together, because there will come a time when he will have to drop and eventually get rid of every player. As Jack Rowell once said when asked what it was like to be a top-flight rugby coach/manager: 'You have fifteen players in a team. Seven hate your guts and the other eight are making up their minds.' That is somewhat of an exaggeration as far as Jack was concerned but there's more than a grain of truth in it.

During my time with England I had the feeling that Jeff Probyn, while he admired Will Carling's technical ability, didn't rate the captain as highly as many other people did. Jeff, I think it is fair to say, didn't warm to Will but fulfilled the criterion of a true team player by having the greatest respect for him. Since Jeff's retirement I have been proved correct, as on numerous occasions he and Will have engaged in verbal battles.

Jeff felt that Will had reached star status and done extremely well out of rugby on the strength of what successive forwards had achieved for England through sweat and toil from the late 1980s onwards. The fact that Will enjoyed fame through appearing on TV in commercials, writing in the press and in general attracting mass-media attention seemed to gall Jeff. Forwards, by the very nature of the job they have to do, rarely look like Tom Cruise or Richard Gere. Will, unlike Jeff, is not a forward and has a certain attractiveness for women and the image-conscious media. In the words of one producer of TV commercials I once met, 'We go for Will because he looks right and is *the* symbol of England's success at rugby.'

Without doubt Will would be the first to deny this. In fact, he would be the first to say that England's record over the years is due to a team effort from the many people involved, both on and off the field.

I don't resent anyone getting on and enjoying commercial success for whatever reason, and furthermore it's not any fault of Will's that the media perceives him to be the most 'saleable and marketable' member of a team. I have done very well out of rugby and I hope that both Will and Jeff go on to reap the benefits of their hard work.

Jeff, great player that he was, delights in rubbing people up the wrong way. The more uptight or upset you get, the more he does it. Sometimes he relishes being downright anti-social, as he was on the outward flight for England's 1988 tour of Australia.

The journey takes twenty-four hours, sometimes longer. As anyone who has made it will testify, it is a tiresome flight with the added problem of jet-lag at the other end.

Some nineteen hours had passed and just about every member of the England team had settled down with a pillow to try to get some sleep. Everyone, that is, except Jeff Probyn.

At Heathrow, while every other member of the England team had bought a newspaper, magazine or book to help them while away the flight, Jeff had bought, of all things, a space invaders game.

For nineteen hours Jeff played this infernal game, to the annoyance of every other player. It involved alien craft coming out of the sky and engaging in crossfire with friendly forces on the ground. The gunfire was represented by a continual 'ping, ping, ping' sound. The alien craft, when hit, nose-dived from the screen with a high-pitched drone, while friendly forces, subjected to a direct hit, exploded with a tinny boom and a succession of rapid high-pitched bleeps.

For every alien craft hit points were scored, only to be reduced every time a friendly craft suffered a similar fate. One thousand points would make Jeff Probyn only a Space Warrior. Two thousand and he'd be a Warlord of the Ancient Skies. He needed 3,000 to become a Teutonic Titan of Termination. The ultimate, however, was to reach 5,000 points, at which point England's thirty-two-year-old premier prop would finally be crowned Kango, King of Cosmic Skies and Protector of Nimbus Nebulla and All Who Dwelleth There.

Ping, ping, ping! Bleep, bleep, bleep. Zurrrrrrrr. Ping,

Ping. Zurrrrrrr. Ping. Zurrrrrrr. Bleep, bleep. Zurrrrrrr! For nineteen hours we had suffered this barrage from Jeff's space invaders. It wasn't so bad when we were all awake, reading, chatting or having a drink with the in-flight meal. But when it came to getting some sleep, the ever-present tinny cosmic racket annoyed every one of us.

'Surely he must be up to 5,000 points by now,' said Wade Dooley, who was sitting next to me.

'I bloody well hope so. It's driving me potty,' I replied.

'And us,' said Stuart Barnes, poking his head through the gap between our seats and pointing to himself and Jon Webb. 'We've been trying to get some shut-eye for the past hour.'

Suddenly the irritating noise stopped. To everyone's relief a blissful peace and quiet descended on the plane and we all settled down in our seats, determined to catch an hour or two of sleep.

Jeff passed by, heading down the aisle towards the rear of the plane.

'He's only stopped because he's gone to the loo.' hissed Stuart.

'Right, that's it!' said Wade, rising and bending forward simultaneously to prevent his 6ft 8in frame coming into contact with the hand-luggage lockers above. 'Let's find that damn thing and hide it.'

There was no sound but the quiet drone of the plane's engines as Wade and I made our way up the aisle to Jeff's seat.

'Where's that 'king game thing?' Wade muttered, rummaging among the papers on Jeff's seat. 'We're going to hide it.'

'Please do,' said a bleary-eyed Simon Halliday, who had the misfortune to be sitting next to Jeff.

Wade found the game and I urged him to hurry up and hide it before Jeff came back to his seat.

Suddenly Wade burst into uncontrollable laughter. His shoulders heaved and his mouth gaped as his mirth became more manic. His left hand, holding the game, fell limply to his side, while his right clutched at his chest. All around us, players started to stir and look up to see what the fuss was about.

'What the hell is up with you?' I asked.

Wade was laughing too much to reply. Braying like a donkey, he fell to his knees as he totally lost control of himself.

'What are you laughing at?' I persisted, ever mindful that Jeff would soon be back.

'What's got hold of him?' Simon asked.

Wade's face, not the most handsome at the best of times, contorted as his guffawing took an even firmer grip on his senses. Unable to speak, he handed the game to me.

Eventually, and only with great effort, he managed to speak. 'How long . . .' Wade struggled to suppress his laughter. 'How long,' he tried again, 'has Jeff been playing with that thing?'

I glanced at my watch. 'Nineteen hours,' I said. 'Ever since we took off from Heathrow.'

'And how many points has he accumulated in that time?'

I looked at the window that displayed the total points tally. 'Forty-seven . . .'

The England skipper on this tour to Australia was Gloucester's John Orwin, who, I have to say, for someone trained in the RAF, did not display brilliant qualities of captaincy. Compare Will Carling or Gavin Hastings. As captains they both show tremendous leadership. In the first Test of the British Lions tour of New Zealand in 1993 the referee controversially disallowed what seemed to be a perfectly good Lions try in the last minute. As a result the Lions lost the game 20–18. That 'perfectly good try' would not only have won the match but, as it turned out, the series. It was a devastating blow to the tourists. To lose in New Zealand is no disgrace but to lose because of the incompetence – or, worse still, bias – of an official most definitely is.

Gavin Hastings was the Lions captain and Will the vice-captain. Bitter and disappointed they must have been but they never showed it. On the contrary, they behaved with dignity and restraint throughout. Neither made his private thoughts and misgivings about the official public knowledge. Both applauded the performance of the All Blacks and, while most Lions players wanted to lynch the Australian official in question, neither Gavin nor Will showed his emotions. Both were wonderful ambassadors for Great Britain and rugby in general.

I have mentioned elsewhere how Donal Lenihan could command respect and rapt attention from a player by simply uttering one sentence. During the British Lions tour of Australia in 1989 Steve Cutler of New South Wales hacked at Donal's ankle during a Wednesday game at Waratah Park in Sydney. Donal simply swung round, raised a finger at Steve and stared at him. He didn't say anything. He didn't have to. He just glared and pointed his finger. The message was received loud and clear and Steve Cutler never had a go at Donal again in that game.

Although John Orwin was a fine player, he possessed neither the gifts of a Hastings or a Carling nor the command of a Donal Lenihan.

The England players were attending a dinner at World Expo '88 in Brisbane. We had played the first Test and lost 16–22. We were in the middle of a punishing schedule of travel, training and games. Even so, the powers that organise tour itineraries, in their infinite wisdom, insisted we attended these formal functions that had little bearing on the players themselves. Tour officials no doubt relish them – they can sip their whiskies and soda or gins and tonic and enjoy the chit-chat, but they don't have to train and play in games as well. Players on tour, irrespective of which of the home countries they are touring with, invariably have too little time off for relaxation between matches.

Imagine such a schedule at home. England play at Twickenham on a Saturday and before their next game the following Saturday they have to play a midweek game, train every day, attend four formal dinners, six press conferences and travel 2,000 miles. It would be ludicrous here, so why is it acceptable abroad?

The Expo '88 dinner over, the players were literally left to twiddle their thumbs as the tour officials chatted to their hosts. A group of us sat talking among ourselves as the dinner tables were cleared. Meanwhile a thoroughly bored Jeff Probyn, on his own, was circling the top of a wine glass with his forefinger and creating a high-pitched whining sound.

After ten minutes or so those within earshot were, not to put too fine a point on it, getting thoroughly pissed off with the noise.

John Orwin marched across to Jeff, determined to put a stop to it. 'Jeff, knock it off. It's getting on everybody's nerves,' he said.

Jeff dutifully stopped and John turned to rejoin the group with whom he had been talking. Before he reached it the whining started again. John swung round and immediately tore a strip off Jeff. 'Jeff, I've told you once; I'm not telling you again! Stop that infernal noise. It's getting on everyone's nerves.'

Jeff stopped again – for all of five seconds. No sooner had John turned to walk away than the noise restarted.

If you know Jeff, you know that when he does such irritating things it's not personal. He does it to everyone at one time or another. He loves winding people up to see how they will react and you always know when he's doing it because of the impish grin. I found the best way to deal with it was to show indifference. Do that and Jeff will soon cease his mind games. John, as England captain, should have made himself familiar with the idiosyncrasies of all his players. It was clear that he hadn't because, far from showing indifference or putting Jeff down with a smart one-liner, he lost control of the situation and himself.

The captain flew into a rage. Jeff, for his part, sat quietly, feet lazily up on a chair, as John went red, then blue, in the face, screaming his displeasure at the prop's behaviour. The longer Jeff sat calmly and quietly, the worse John's tantrum became. In the end he was yelling at the top of his voice, wisps of saliva flying from his mouth. 'I'm sending you home on the next flight!' he finished hysterically as the entire room looked on.

'That's it!' John said, eyes wide open, a finger raised in the air as if he had suddenly come up with the solution to the problem. 'Yes! I'm sending you home on the next flight. As soon as you get back to the hotel I want you to pack your bag!'

We all looked on in embarrassed silence. As I said to Wade Dooley at the time, 'John's lost it.' Under pressure he had flipped. Heaven knows what Rory Underwood, a fellow RAF officer, thought of the incident. John's outburst was not in keeping with what one expects from an England captain, never mind someone with a responsible position in the RAF. John eventually calmed down and Jeff, of course, was not sent home on the next flight. Just as well, as we would have been a laughing stock and the press would have had a field day. Imagine the headlines:

PROBYN GOES DOWN IN RUGBY FOLK 'LOIRE'.

CAPTAIN'S WHINE AT WINE GLASS – PROBYN HOME!

For all he could annoy you, I liked Jeff. As a team-mate on the pitch you knew you could rely on him and he wouldn't flinch an inch when it got rough. I never rose to the bait when Jeff played his little mind games, and he never sought me out for special treatment.

To my knowledge there have been only two incidents when Jeff's forthright views and irascibility have backfired on him. During that Australian tour of 1988 England played an Australian President's XV. Jeff was on the bench as a replacement and throughout the game he badgered referee Byres. He was forever calling out that one Australian player or another was offside. When the referee gave an England player offside, on the other hand, Jeff would scream that he was blind and had made yet another bad decision.

Ten minutes remained when the referee halted an England surge forward from a ruck by giving me offside.

'Ridiculous decision!' shouted Jeff from the dug-out. 'Coochie was never offside!'

The referee blew his whistle to stop the President's side restarting the game and made his way over to the England bench. We all expected him to take issue with manager Geoff Cooke about the sledging he was receiving from Jeff. Instead he indicated that the England replacements should make room for him on the bench. Byres squeezed himself between Jeff Probyn and Simon Halliday.

'What the hell are you doing, ref?' Jeff asked, taken aback.

'Well, sport,' said Mr Byres. 'Seems to me you get a perfect view of the game from here.'

I mentioned earlier how up to date Jeff is with the latest in technological advances and thinking, yet how he can be curiously out of step with other modern developments. Never was this better demonstrated than when he appeared on BBC's *Rugby Special* programme in November 1994 and said that women had no place in rugby. Jeff even went as far as to say that a woman's place was in the home, cooking and so on. As soon as he said it I cringed, knowing hands would be reaching for pens.

I hope women do not take Jeff's view as being representative of the majority of us involved in the game. I welcome women in rugby, as players, officials and supporters. Why not a woman in the hierarchy of the RFU? Women have tried, but at the time of writing the RFU say you have to be eligible to play for England in order to be eligible for the committee. It all sounds like male chauvinism to me and I think women should enjoy equality in rugby as in every other area of society.

The Women's World Championships in Edinburgh in April 1994 showed just how strong the women's game is and the matches also produced some scintillating rugby of a very good standard. If Jeff had seen England captain Gill Burns leading England in their 38–23 win over the USA in the final, he might have thought twice before making such a statement on television. As it was, Jeff went on the nation's prime rugby TV programme with a bull-in-a-china-shop attitude and was rightly pilloried for his outdated views.

The next time Jeff appeared on *Rugby Special* he was seen coaching a women's team at Richmond and being rather patronising about the standard. Women's rugby does not want to be patronised. It simply wants to be supported and I, for one, give it my wholehearted support, as I do rugby at all levels and in all spheres throughout the world.

Jeff popped up again on the same programme a month or so later and was very careful about what he said. He played it completely safe. What a shame! People like Jeff make great TV when they are being irascible and irritating. Such outspoken and controversial viewpoints stir up emotions and provoke reactions in viewers, which can only be healthy for rugby or whatever other subject is being debated. Unfortunately, they are a rarity. Most TV pundits are as dull as chalk.

When I watched Jeff make those comments about women

and rugby my mind immediately went back to the space invaders game and the wine glass. I didn't take what he said about women in rugby too seriously. I recognised a certain impish grin.

32

Dewi Morris

THE 1995 World Cup in South Africa was the swansong in the career of my good friend Dewi Morris.

Dewi was never one of the England glamour boys but his all-out approach and never-say-die attitude turned him into a comic-book-type hero for thousands of rugby fans.

Between 1992 and 1995 Dewi was, to my mind, England's most underrated player. He possessed that most important quality of any good scrum-half, the ability to pass the ball quickly and accurately to both right and left. When he was a young boy in Wales, for it was there that he was born, he was crossing a field when a herd of bulls ran towards him and flattened him. Undeterred, Dewi got back on his feet and continued on his way. I suppose it was this incident that first put the idea in his head that he had all the makings of a good scrum-half.

You can't hide on a rugby pitch at scrum-half — not that Dewi would ever think of doing such a thing. Like all good scrum-halves, he was the pivot from which every move began.

Dewi began his career with Winnington Park and arrived at Orrell via Liverpool St Helens. He showed what can be achieved when aspiration, motivation and skill are fuelled by an indomitable spirit. In consequence he is a suitable role model for any ambitious young player.

Towards the end of his playing career Dewi started out on the after-dinner circuit. He worked hard at his after-dinner speech and delivery, like he did on his rugby, never accepting second-best. Now he's one of the funniest and most accomplished speakers on the circuit and I hope he goes on successfully for many years.

My favourite story about Dewi took place after we had played in the 1989 11–0 win over France at Twickenham. After the formal dinner in the evening we England players celebrated our victory in the lounge bar of our hotel until nigh on four in the morning.

Joining our celebrations was the former Harlequins full-back Bob Hiller, who himself won nineteen caps for England. It's a little-known fact but following a game, when he's relaxing with a pint, Dewi likes a cigarette. During the course of the night he'll smoke just the one and, strangely, won't indulge again until after the next match.

The jollities were swimming along wonderfully well and Dewi produced his one cigarette. As none of the other players smoked, he went in search of a light and caught sight of Bob Hiller, who was propping up the bar, playing with one of the hotel's complimentary books of matches and then popping it into his jacket pocket. 'Have you got a light, please?' Dewi asked, holding up the ciga-rette.

'Sorry, no I haven't,' said Bob.

'You're Bob Hiller, aren't you?' asked Dewi.

'Yes.'

'People tell me you're a very friendly and caring person. I've got to say, I'm a bit disappointed in your attitude,' said Dewi, miffed.

'How d'you mean?' asked Bob, who still hadn't produced the matches from his pocket.

'Well, I asked you politely for a light and you told me you didn't have one. But I just saw you put a book of matches into your jacket pocket.'

'That just shows how friendly and caring I am,' said Bob. 'How's that?' asked Dewi, puzzled.

'Well, if I gave you a light for that cigarette, you might feel obliged to offer me one and I'd smoke it. Then, when I light up, I'd feel obliged to offer you one and we'd end up in conversation and offering one another cigarettes. Then you'd feel obliged to buy me a drink the next time you wanted a pint.'

'Yes. So?' Dewi said, seeing nothing wrong with such social behaviour.

'Well, I'd then feel obliged to buy you a drink. Then you'd buy me one and so we would go on all evening, buying each other drinks. Then, at the end of the night, you'd tell me you had nowhere to stay in London and, as we have spent the evening in one another's company, I'd feel obliged to invite you back to our house.'

Dewi kept nodding his head, trying to keep track of Bob's explanation.

'Thing is,' continued Bob, 'we have only two bedrooms. My wife and I sleep in one and my nineteen-year-old daughter sleeps in the other. Now, she's very curvaceous and beautiful and you, being a young lad, would give in to your basic instincts. Next thing we know, she'd be pregnant and you'd tell me you wouldn't marry her.'

'But I would, I would!' claimed Dewi earnestly.

'You don't have to,' said Bob, calm and casual. 'Because I'm not going to give you a light.'

33

Fun and Games

As I've recounted elsewhere in this book, for more than a decade Bath has enjoyed considerable success. According to some in the press, much of this is due to Bath's policy of recruiting top international players. Complete and utter garbage!

In 1995 we had over a dozen capped players at Bath, of whom only Tony Swift and Ireland's Simon Geoghegan were internationals prior to joining us. The same applies if you look back over that golden period of 1984 to 1994. Bath always had ten or so internationals on the books at any given time, yet in all that time only two, Stuart Barnes from Bristol and Tony, who joined us from Swansea, had played international rugby before coming to the Rec.

The standard set for players at Bath is so high that it equates with international rugby. That is why when someone plays regularly for the first XV he inevitably comes under the scrutiny of the international selectors. Bath has turned many a player, myself included, into an international. We do not consciously go out and sign established internationals.

I have also mentioned elsewhere how ruthless and deter- mined Jack Rowell was to bring success to Bath. In time this thirst for success rubbed off on each and every player. Jack's direct approach meant he told players exactly what he thought of them. When full-back Jon Webb arrived at Bath from local rivals Bristol, he lacked self-belief and motivation. Jack knew that Webby had ability all right, and he felt he could get him to demonstrate it.

Jack wasted no time in candidly telling Webby exactly what was wrong with his game and why he wasn't doing the business on the park. At the time Jon didn't like what Jack was telling him but, as well as being hyper-critical, Jack was also constructive, telling Webby precisely what he had to do if he wanted to continue playing top-class rugby. It was exactly what the player needed. Jon's game had been allowed to drift and deteriorate and he needed someone to spend time with him and show a genuine interest in it.

His game improved in leaps and bounds and he retired a top-level international full-back. It was Jack at his best: he had created a community and a team at Bath, but he also recognised that his players were individuals.

I heard one pundit on Radio 5 say that Jack Rowell ruled by fear at Bath. That's garbage as well. No coach, no matter how good, will get his players to play out of their skins for him by bullying them. Besides, can you imagine anyone ever bullying the likes of me, David Egerton, Graham Dawe, Nigel Redman, Victor Ubogu or Jon Hall? Yet I still hear that 'fear' theory being put forward – though never by anyone who played for Jack.

We may well have taken our rugby more seriously than any other club in the land but that is not to say we didn't have fun. We did, and plenty of it, too.

Lambridge, the Bath training ground where our second and third XVs play, is situated on London Road, which runs east out of Bath city centre towards the A46. The houses on London Road near Lambridge are grand

affairs, set back off the road, some of them three sto-
reys high.

In 1985 a friend of Richard Hill's bought one of the houses
yards from Lambridge. In the summer he gave Richard a key
and asked him to keep an eye on the place while he went
on holiday with his fiancée, whom he was due to marry in
September.

While his friend was away Richard had a copy of the key
made and kept it when he returned the original. Come
September, when Richard's friend went out on his stag night,
Richard enlisted the help of me, Graham Dawe, Greg Bess,
Jon Hall and John Palmer.

While Richard's friend was out on his stag night, we went
to the house, removed all the furniture and stored it safely at
Lambridge. We took up all the carpets and laid down turf in
every room, including the hall, stairs and landing. For effect
we also brought in four sheep and let them graze to their
hearts' content.

The gag nearly backfired. When Richard's friend returned,
somewhat the worse for beer, in the early hours and switched
on the light the scene that greeted him was such a shock to
his system that he fainted.

After our 15–12 win over Harlequins in the Pilkington
Cup final in 1992, a reporter remarked to Jack Rowell that
this was his seventh Pilkington Cup success in nine years.
'You've been lucky at Bath in the past ten years or so,
haven't you?' he said.

'It's bloody funny,' replied Jack, 'but the harder the players
and I work, the luckier we seem to get.'

The larger-than-life characters in the dressing-room made
for a good life at the club; the fact that we were successful as
well made it a great one. Roger Spurrell likes his Guinness.
In 1987 we played Leicester at home and Roger was chatting
in the bar to their captain, Paul Dodge. As captains do, they

were swapping notes on the various opposition they had come up against that season and Roger mentioned the previous week, when Bath had visited London Irish and he had spent a most convivial evening with the Irish lads imbibing Guinness.

'The London Irish lads drink it as if Guinness needed the barrels back,' remarked Paul.

'Incidentally,' said Roger, 'do you know in which month of the year the Irish drink the least Guinness?'

Paul replied that he didn't.

'They told me February,' said Roger in all seriousness.

Bath has always welcomed, indeed encouraged, the wives and girlfriends of the players to be part and parcel of club life. As Jack Rowell used to tell us: 'Anyone who is unhappy with his partner is not going to be a happy player. Full stop!' Jack always made a fuss of our partners when they came to the ground, and quite right, too.

In 1990 we beat arch-rivals Gloucester 6–3 in a closely fought game to reach the Pilkington Cup final. Back at the Rec we were all celebrating in style with our wives and girlfriends. Our captain, Stuart Barnes, was chatting to one of our supporters and offered to buy him a drink. 'What would you like?' he asked.

'Me?' said the supporter, surprised but pleased as punch to be bought a drink by the Bath captain. 'I'd like something tall, cold and full of gin.'

'Then come and meet the wife!' said Stuart.

Rugby has always been associated with a good social life and that, of course, means a liking for alcohol in its many forms. During our 1986 pre-season tour of Scotland, Bath played two games against Select XVs on a short tour of the Borders before getting down to the serious business of the Courage Leagues.

Jack Rowell didn't want us to have too rigorous an outing before the start of the season proper, so the two Select

XVs were drawn from the minor clubs in the area. We knew we would easily win both games, though the results were not important. These two matches would be useful 'leg-stretchers' at this early stage and would allow Jack to try one or two tactical things in a real game situation. The idea was also that we would build up from these two matches by playing gradually stronger opposition in order peak for the opening of the Courage League One programme.

A Bath XV, a mixture of players from our first and second teams, played against a Representative XV from Border clubs. Ten minutes from the end I had a head-on collision with the Representative prop Ian McKay, who played his rugby with a team from near Dalbeattie.

McKay ended up out cold on the pitch and I immediately signalled for his side's doctor to come out on to the field and attend to him.

First aid administered, McKay regained consciousness but had to be carried off on a stretcher by St John Ambulance personnel. 'Get him into the changing-room and give him a few drams of whisky,' the doctor told the senior of four St John men.

'You don't know him. He might be a teetotaller,' I said, only partly in jest.

The doctor turned to me. 'In that case he wouldnae be worth saving!'

34

Influence

BEING IN the limelight can have its advantages and disadvantages. I once met a famous rock star at a party who told me that one of the prices of fame was that he could no longer pop into the local video shop and take out an adult X-rated video!

Fame, as I have said on many an occasion, will trip you up if you ever take it, or yourself, too seriously. Even if you don't, it can still play nasty tricks on you.

In 1993 I attended a rugby dinner in Abertillery in Gwent. I arrived at the hotel where I was staying at the same time as the great former Welsh international of the 1970s Derek Quinnell, also father of Scott (who at the time was still with Llanelli, though he later went on to Rugby League).

As we checked in, Derek was pleasantly surprised by the reaction of the hotel receptionist.

'Not *the* Mr Quinnell?' she asked.

'Why, yes – I'm Derek Quinnell who used to play for Llanelli,' replied Derek, blushing.

The receptionist's face fell and her tone of voice betrayed her obvious disappointment. 'Ah,' she said, 'I thought you might have been Scott's father.'

The Irish politician Dick Spring was walking through Dublin with Premier Albert Reynolds in 1993, after they had formed a coalition government. As the two most powerful men in Ireland at the time strolled together through St Stephen's Green, passer-by after passer-by said hello to Dick, but not to the Prime Minister.

'It's odd that so many people are saying hello to me,' said Dick.

'That's because you're famous,' replied Albert Reynolds.

'But you're our Prime Minister,' Dick pointed out.

'Ah, that's true,' said Reynolds, 'but I never played rugby for Ireland.'

Like a little knowledge, a little fame can be a dangerous thing; but not if you recognise it for not being much in the first place. Still, even a little fame can bring influence, as was the case with my pal Jon Hall, the former Bath captain.

After Courage League games the Bath players enjoy a few drinks in one of the bars at the Rec, then, more often than not, drift away in groups to one restaurant or another. After we beat Gloucester 46–17 in 1993, Jon, Richard Hill, Stuart Barnes, Andy Robinson, Phil de Glanville and I and our respective partners decided to go to an Indian restaurant in Bath called the Eastern Eye. A lot of people were talking about the place, so rather than risk arriving on spec late in the evening, I rang the restaurant as soon as the game ended to reserve a table for twelve.

As I returned to the home-team dressing-room, Jon asked me what time the table had been booked for.

'Ten o'clock,' I said.

'Ten?' said Jon. 'We don't want to be eating that late.'

'It's the earliest they could fit us in,' I explained. 'After all, it is a Saturday night.'

Jon finished dressing and was adamant he could get an earlier booking. We followed him to the phone and listened as he spoke the restaurant. 'Hello, Eastern Eye? My friend just spoke to you to book a table for twelve and he was told the earliest was ten o'clock. Is there any possibility you could fit us in earlier? My name? Jon Hall. Yes, it is . . . Jon Hall the captain of Bath rugby team . . .'

Jon gave the impression of being all bashful, but he was pleased that his name was achieving the desired result.

'No, no, no, I couldn't let you do that . . . No, it's very good of you, but really . . . Well, I don't want you to think just because it is me on the phone that I'm expecting any special treatment . . . Well, if you insist it is no trouble to you, that would be wonderful, the earlier the better, really, only ten is too late to eat . . . Fine, fine . . . Thank you ever so much. Thank you!'

Jon replaced the receiver and turned round beaming. 'There!' he said proudly. 'Nothing to it. My name carries a bit of weight around here. Eating at ten o'clock, my foot.'

We all stood around, impressed by Jon's influence.

'What time have they managed to fit us in, then?' I asked.

'Nine-fifty,' he said triumphantly.

The Game Then, Now and in the Future

'It's not as if it's a great discovery. There's money everywhere in rugby now and it's time to stop the hypocrisy.'

Pierre Berbizier, France coach.

'For some, a good kick up the backside can be an enlightening experience.'

Gavin Hastings, Watsonians, Scotland and British Lions.

35

Planet Rugby

R UGBY IS a game of opinions. Many are the hours that have
been spent in the dressing-room, on a coach journey home
or propping up some club's bar in heated debate of one aspect
or another of the game. One thing everyone does seem to agree
upon, however, is that rugby is growing.

The incredible changes seen throughout the game, from top
to bottom, since 1987 have resulted in a massive growth of
interest in the sport, not only within the major International
Board countries but throughout the world.

The 1995 Rugby World Cup proved the most successful
yet, and I think future World Cups will go from strength
to strength. Recently we have seen the emergence of Fiji,
Tonga, Zimbabwe, Western Samoa, Italy, Japan, Romania,
Canada and Argentina as teams capable of playing good
rugby and competing with the major IB countries. I refer
to them as the 'second division' of international rugby. And
the growth of those countries in rugby terms is just the
tip of the iceberg. Travelling the world I have seen the
game growing rapidly in countries across every continent.
It will be only a matter of time before what you might
call the 'third division' of international rugby can compete

with the more established nations – provided it is allowed to develop, that is.

In Europe, for instance, Belgium has a national league and cup that are well established and senior clubs have grown in number to sixty-five. The game is also growing in Germany, Holland, Poland, Portugal, Spain and Russia. In Europe it is not unusual to find a sporting club which has a number of teams playing different sports under its banner. In Portugal the famous soccer clubs Benfica and Sporting Lisbon have rugby teams, as does 1878 Hanover in Germany.

Spain now boasts 236 senior clubs in a union that is superbly run and administered. If I were asked to predict which country would be next to make the breakthrough into top-class international rugby, I would say Spain. There is, of course, a proliferation of clubs in the north, close to the rugby hotbed of the south of France, but the game is now growing generally across the country. The Five Nations tournament is now regularly screened on Spanish TV and the fact that Spain narrowly missed qualifying from their European Zone group for the 1995 World Cup bodes well for the future.

Elsewhere in Europe, in 1994–5 Denmark restructured its rugby and now has a first division fed by regional leagues in Jutland, Fyn and Zeeland. In 1994 Sweden formed a three-division national league operating promotion and relegation, also fed by regional leagues. Standards are improving and we are starting to see the first Scandinavian players arriving in Great Britain to try their hand at top-class rugby. The most notable import to date is Kari Tapper, the Swedish number 8 who has signed for Aberavon and has played for the Barbarians.

In Africa rugby is beginning to take a foothold, and not just in the south. African rugby has always been influenced by the French in the north of the continent and by South Africa in the south. Now, however, we are seeing countries such as Zambia, Ivory Coast, Kenya, Tanzania, Uganda, Ghana and

Nigeria emerging to challenge Morocco and Tunisia in the north and, to a lesser extent, the all-powerful South Africa and Zimbabwe in the south.

Lack of finance and facilities and the vast distances teams have to travel for games are a stumbling block to the game's development in that continent. For these reasons I think the growth of the sport in Africa will be slower. I can't see it blossoming in the same way as it is doing in continental Europe or the Far East. What will be interesting, though, as we enter the twenty-first century, is the development of the game in the black townships of South Africa. With equal opportunities I am sure we will see the emergence of black players in integrated teams. We should also see an increase in South African club teams as more and more young black players take up the game. The money seems to be there to help development and, like him or loathe him, Louis Luyt from Transvaal, who to all intents and purposes runs South African rugby, did secure a sponsorship deal in 1994 for the South African RFU worth 96 million rand over six years. I just hope that large chunks of that will be used to improve facilities and develop the game in the townships.

It was Luyt who in 1971 tried to get the first South African multi-racial sports event off the ground, and who in 1969 called for blacks and coloureds to be given the vote. In the eighties he supported the campaign to release the imprisoned Nelson Mandela, so it is to be hoped that money will be forthcoming for the expansion of rugby in the deprived townships. In 1995 Luyt sanctioned 3 million rand for the development of multi-racial rugby in the Transvaal alone. So while there is a still long way to go, there are grounds for optimism.

In the Far East the annual Hong Kong Sevens is now one of the major tournaments in the rugby calendar. Rugby in Hong Kong goes far beyond the world's premier sevens tournament, however. They have ten senior clubs, each with over 200 players. As in Japan, the big problem in Hong Kong is finding land for pitches. The game has also been introduced across the border in China and first signs are that the Chinese people like what they have seen. Par for the course — you see one Chinese game of rugby and two hours later you want to watch another!

Thailand, Papua New Guinea, Taiwan, Singapore and Malaysia all have growing national competitions but the country I believe has witnessed the most rapid development is South Korea.

It was the South Koreans who pushed for rugby to be included in the Olympics. They failed by only two votes. After they won the Asian Championship in 1991, interest in rugby in the country mushroomed and they now boast a highly competitive league of fourteen clubs. The sport is by no means as popular as soccer, baseball or volleyball, but it is definitely growing. The armed forces have joined the universities in taking up rugby and recent victories over Japan and Western Samoa indicate that it will be only a matter of time before the South Koreans are regulars on the international scene.

Of all the countries in the East, none has such a rugby history as India. It's a throwback to the days of the empire, of course. India formed its board as long ago as 1874 and lays claim to being the oldest overseas union. I have mentioned the history of the Calcutta Cup, competed for annually by Scotland and England, but there is also another Calcutta Cup, the premier cup tournament in Indian rugby, which was introduced in 1978. Rugby is not as popular as cricket or hockey with the Indian people but, with 9,000 players and 160 clubs, it is on a par with soccer and development is healthy. A mark of the growth in its popularity is that over 27,000 people turned out to watch an international between India and Japan in 1994, compared with fewer than a thousand for a match between the same two countries in 1979.

A few years back we had an Indian player in our Under-21

side at Bath. Kapil Singh was studying at Bristol University and rugby was his main sport. In the summer we fixed him up with a job working on the canals. From that point on he became known as the Onion Bargee.

As for the Americas, rugby is already well established in Argentina in the south and in Canada and the USA in the north of the continent. However, Brazil, Chile, Paraguay and Uruguay compete in the South American Championship and all have taken heart from Canada's excellent performance in beating Wales in Cardiff in 1993 and their track record in the World Cup, particularly that of 1991, in which they reached the quarter-finals. The Pumas of Argentina apart, Chile seem to be making most headway on this continent. Their league system boasts just under a hundred teams and, with estimates of between 6,000 and 10,000 people playing the game every weekend, the Chileans may soon be on a par with the Pumas.

It would be a tremendous fillip to rugby in general if the home unions sent touring teams to these developing rugby countries, say at B or Under-21 levels, even if just for a mini-tour of two or three games. It would be good for home-grown players to see these countries and experience the rugby being played there, and the benefits to the hosts of such games, and perhaps of coaching sessions with top-class players, could be incalculable. If the powers that be really want to see their sport grow into a world game that people of all nations and cultures love and enjoy, why don't they organise such tours?

Each Rugby World Cup is more successful than the last and the 1995 tournament in South Africa made millions of pounds for the leading unions. While the game must constantly be developed at home, couldn't some of this money be used to improve facilities in some of the nations I have mentioned? The squabbling among union officials during the World Cup in

Great Britain and France in 1991, when officials bickered about trivia, was shameful. Their behaviour made a mockery of the spirit in which the players played and the spectators supported the games.

On the subject of priorities I recently met an official from the Brazilian RFU at a rugby dinner. 'In Brazil our problem is money. We are a soccer-mad country but not every boy will play soccer for Brazil or a top club,' he explained. 'The chances of a boy doing that at rugby is far greater but we need money to provide better facilities to attract youngsters in the first place.'

'Can you not ask for grants or loans?' I asked.

'Listen,' said the official, with a world-weary look on his face. 'Brazil is really a Third World country.'

'I appreciate that the gulf between the small group who are rich and the masses who are poor is immense. But your sports minister, Pele, is a soccer legend. What finer ambassador for Brazilian rugby could you have than Pele? As a sportsman he is known, respected and trusted throughout the world.'

He nodded. 'How did you buy your house, Mr Chilcott?' he asked.

'With a mortgage. I borrowed the money from a building society.'

'Building society or bank, same thing,' he said. 'Banks borrow from the national bank, in your case the Bank of England. National banks borrow from governments. Governments borrow from organisations like the EC or IMF, who, in turn, borrow it from rich countries like Switzerland or Germany. They borrow from multi-national companies such as Brazilian Oil, who are billions and billions of dollars in debt. But to whom? Whom did *they* borrow it from?'

I said I had no idea.

'Nor me,' he said. 'Now, in such a complicated web of

international financial intrigue, who do you think is going to find money to lend to us to develop rugby in Brazil?'

I took his point but I still believe it is down to the fat-cat full International Board unions.

Of course, there may be people in such unions who do not want to see rugby develop to the stage where such countries are competing on a par with England, Scotland, France, New Zealand or Australia. They see what has happened to England in soccer – the countries to which we introduced the game have caught up and overtaken us, and the power balance of international soccer has therefore shifted. Afraid of losing their own power base, certain unions and officials may be paying only lip-service to developing the game worldwide. I hope this is not the case. If such a thing were proved, it would surpass all previous rugby scandals.

I am a regular visitor to the Middle East, both to speak and with the rugby theatre show I do with the former Scottish international and British Lion Gordon Brown, the brilliant sporting impressionist Mike Osman and my co-author on this book, the versatile writer/comic Les Scott. Interest in rugby in this part of the world is phenomenal, and not just among ex-pats. The strength and standard of play in the Gulf League continues to improve, with Bahrain, Oman, Dubai, Qatar, Sharjah, Abu Dhabi and Muscat leading the way.

The Dubai Sevens has grown in stature and is now accepted as a top international tournament. While the ex-pats from Great Britain, New Zealand, Australia and France may encounter one or two discrepancies in local licensing laws, rugby is very much part of the rapidly expanding Middle East sporting scene.

Although I cannot envisage Qatar or Abu Dhabi competing on level terms in the near future against what I have called second-division international teams such as Italy or Western Samoa, never mind any of the full Board countries, the prospect of a combined Gulf States side doing so is not beyond the realms of possibility.

In 1993 I accepted an invitation to speak to the members of the Royal State Oil Club of Oman. It was to be a quick in-and-out job. I'd fly in, speak to the club members at their entertainment night and then fly straight back home again. The function was to start at 5 p.m. local time and my flight from Heathrow was due to arrive in Muscat at 2 p.m., which should have given me more than enough time to wash and change before the dinner, had not the flights out of Heathrow been delayed. We touched down at Muscat at 4.50.

Hot, bothered, flustered and anxious, I stepped out of the airport and made my way over to a row of taxis. 'Is it far to the Royal State Oil Club?' I asked one taxi driver.

'No. Ten, fifteen minutes at the most,' he replied.

I heaved a sigh of relief. With the dinner starting at five, they would not be expecting me to entertain them until after six. It would give me enough time to wash and change.

'There's a big entertainment function taking place at the club,' I said to the taxi driver. 'Can you take me there?'

'Of course, sir. No problem,' he said.

Even though the car was air-conditioned, the heat was intense and, after the long wait at Heathrow and the flight itself, it was all I could do to stop myself nodding off. After ten minutes or so I gave in to my tiredness and fell asleep.

What must have been a bump in the road jolted the taxi and awoke me. I glanced lazily down at my watch and sat bolt upright, rubbing my face. I was riddled with panic when a look at the clock on the car's dashboard confirmed the time on my watch. It was 6.15.

'Is that clock right?' I asked, all flustered.

'Yes, sir. Very accurate,' said the driver.

'Quarter past six!' I shouted aloud. 'When I got into this taxi you said it was only fifteen minutes at most to the Royal

State Oil Club. We've been driving for an hour and twenty minutes already. Where the hell are you taking me?'

'You want entertainment, sir? I take you to a club owned by my brother-in-law, other side of Matrah,' he said, smiling at me through his rear-view mirror. 'Much better than the Royal State Oil Club. Besides, they've got that English rugby player Gareth Chilcott performing tonight. Very boring for you!'

36

Gonna Make You a Star?

I MENTIONED earlier the marvellous film *This Sporting Life*. Richard Harris, who plays the part of Harry Machin, the king-pin of the City Rugby League club, is introduced to Mrs Weaver, the wife of the club chairman.

'I've not met a star before,' says Mrs Weaver.

'We don't have stars in this sport,' replies Harris. 'That's soccer.'

That may well have been the case back in 1963 but nowadays soccer is not the only sport to have 'stars'. In recent years, with increased television exposure of top games and the opportunity for rugby players to rub shoulders with famous people from other sports on television programmes such as *A Question of Sport*, the age of the rugby superstar has arrived.

I have always thought of my TV and theatre appearances as a bonus to my job as commercial manager and co-coach at Bath. Some rugby players, however, receive invitations to appear as summarisers and pundits on BBC TV's Five Nations coverage or *Rugby Special* and immediately think, 'Here's an opportunity to make a TV career.' More often than not they do not want to upset anyone or to jeopardise future TV opportunites, so they reply in the blandest manner to the questions put to them. It's safe TV but it is often boring.

The former Scottish international Gordon Brown sees TV work in much the same way as I do, as a bonus; neither of us thinks of it in terms of paying the mortgage. As a consequence we're more relaxed about such appearances and not afraid to speak our minds or to take a contrary point of view, often to each other. Producers tell Gordon and me that it makes for better and more entertaining television. I'd like to think so. Next time you watch BBC's *Rugby Special*, count the number of times anchorman John Inverdale makes a point to a studio guest only for the guest to reply, 'Yes, that's right.'

The new look given to *Rugby Special* when the independent company Chrysalis took over from the BBC included a theme tune and opening sequence out of keeping with a game that is fast, exciting and skilful. John Inverdale, however laudable his intentions in wearing a shirt from a different club every week, looked like a loafer from some public bar instead of a TV presenter exuding expertise and authoritative comment.

The 'A to Z of Rugby' featured in that series had a voice-over by a young woman. Nothing wrong with that, of course, if we had heard of the lady in question and she was recognised as being knowledgeable about rugby. But no one knew who she was, so when she explained such matters as the various forms of attack in rugby her comments had no authority. It would have been better to have called in someone like Bill Beaumont, Ian McGeechan or a player such as Dewi Morris.

That said, *Rugby Special* does marvellous work in covering all aspects of the game, unlike soccer's *Match of the Day*. I particularly like the exposure it gives the grass roots and women's rugby, two burgeoning areas of the game. Its coverage of the top-class games in England, Wales and Scotland is comprehensive. The production facilities and editing involved in bringing us the highlights and tries from so many games every weekend must be phenomenal and, when all is said and done, it is *the* programme for rugby fans. Whoever recognised that there was a large audience wanting a weekly rugby magazine programme deserves another credit. I hope *Rugby Special* goes from strength to strength. Minor faults apart, it does a great job, not only in reporting rugby but in enhancing the general profile of our game – and that of people like me!

I like being in the public eye but I always remember that fame can disappear as quickly as it arrived. As my TV appearances become more frequent and my press coverage more widespread, I try to keep my feet firmly on the ground. I once heard Cliff Richard asked how he had managed to survive so long in the pop business and remain a down-to-earth, easy-going guy. He replied, 'Because I have never, ever believed my own publicity.' Sound advice from someone who has been at the forefront of the public's attention for nigh on forty years.

I welcome the increased interest in and publicity for my sport. The profile of the game has grown incredibly in recent years and, along with this, players such as Will Carling, Rory Underwood, Jerry Guscott and Rob Andrew have not only become household names but fine ambassadors for rugby. Through my easily recognisable physique and, TV, theatre and after-dinner work, I too now enjoy a degree of limelight in the wake of my retirement from playing. As I have said, my feet are firmly planted on the ground but, should they ever rise a fraction, I know I can count on family, friends and the public to bring me back down to earth, as one old lady did in a Bristol supermarket in December 1994.

My wife Ann had taken our daughter Chloe Christmas shopping. I had spent the day at work at the Recreation Ground and had popped into the supermarket on the way home to pick up one or two items we needed.

I was pushing a trolley around the aisles when I noticed this elderly lady looking at me with a somewhat mystified expression. At first I took little notice but, as the old dear continued to stare at me, I felt compelled to say hello. She didn't reply but simply carried on scrutinising my face.

As is often the case in supermarkets, after you have said hello to someone you then keep meeting them in every aisle you walk down, creating the awkward situation of whether or not you should speak to them again. On this occasion in every aisle I chose I passed the same lady and, although I offered her a polite if somewhat embarrassed smile each time I met her, she just stared back at me again with a puzzled look on her face.

I was reaching into the frozen-foods section when a thin, wrinkled hand touched my arm. 'Excuse me, but I'm not mistaken am I?'

'Mistaken?' I asked, turning to see the elderly lady yet again.

'It is *you*, isn't it? Only I would never expect to see you shopping in here.'

Only the previous week I had appeared in the BBC drama series *Casualty* and on Channel 4's *Big Breakfast*. Naturally I was pleased to be recognised. 'Yes, it is me,' I said, beaming and waiting for the paper and pen to be produced for my autograph.

The woman screwed up her face in annoyance and, wagging her finger at me, asked: 'Right, then. When are you coming back to finish that tiling in my bathroom?'

Nowadays rugby is producing new stars all the time. Bath's Ben Clarke is a prime example. Having won his first cap as recently as 1992, and already a fixture in the England team and a British Lion to boot, Ben is a back-row forward of whom we still have to see the best. His height, muscular physique and handsome good looks make him popular with the ladies, and tackles such as the one with which he hit John Kirwan in the Lions' second

Test against the All Blacks ensure that opponents don't readily forget him, either.

Such were Ben's performances against New Zealand in 1993 that they moved the great former All Black Colin 'Pinetree' Meads to say: 'Take the rest home but leave Clarke here.' It's easier to get an All Black to knit with sawdust than to pay a compliment to a member of the opposition and praise from Colin is praise indeed.

Ben had a difficult act to follow in the England team when he was asked to replace Peter Winterbottom at open side. His natural game is really at No. 8, and many a player would have complained that he could not do himself justice playing out of position. Not so Ben. He simply got on with the job in hand and his total commitment and renowned athleticism ensured that he shone in whichever position he was asked to fill.

Ben joined Bath from Saracens and is a prime case of a young player who has progressed through the ranks of junior rugby. He began playing with the Colts at Bishop's Stortford, where his father is the club chairman.

Ben may be a rising star but, like the other players at Bath, he will jump at the chance of helping out in the local community when asked. Following our 21–9 victory over Leicester in the 1994 Pilkington Cup final, we arrived back in Bath to a civic reception and a tumultuous welcome from the people of the city. Ever mindful that we had won the cup for the people of our town, we wanted to visit as many local community groups as possible to show them at first hand the prestigious trophy we had once again won for them at Twickenham.

One evening Ben, Tony Swift, Victor Ubogu and I took the Pilkington Cup to a home for the elderly which offered specialist care to those suffering from senile dementia.

A number of the ladies 'cooed and ah'd' when it was Ben's turn to be introduced and, once the formalities were over, we wandered about chatting to these lovely folk and showing off the cup and our winners' medals.

I was chatting to an old gentleman when Ben settled down next to us to talk to a thin, drawn lady who, up to that point, had not said a word. As he made polite conversation the lady stared blankly into his face. It was obvious she didn't have a clue who he was or what we were doing there. 'Do you know who I am?' asked Ben eventually in a gentle voice.

'No,' said the old dear. 'But if you go and ask Matron she'll tell you. She's knows everyone in here.'

As I say, if you ever get any high-falutin' ideas about your status as a personality, you can always rely on someone to bring you back to reality.

37

Sketches From My Notebook

B ATH RFC might be the most successful club side in the
world but for me it is the greatest club for many reasons
apart from silverware won. The friendliness, the fun and the
dressing-room camaraderie combine to make me view Bath as
my 'other family'.

Playing for the club gave me tremendous pleasure and great
times and I count myself lucky to be still involved with the club
now, as a co-coach to Brian Ashton and also as commercial
manager. My playing days might be over, bar the odd charity
game, but what no one can take away is a treasure trove of great
memories. Throughout my career I jotted down in notebooks
details of games, incidents and anecdotes from my times with
Bath and England. Looking back at those notes when I sat down
to write this book only emphasised to me what great fun it all
was. Here are some examples from my notebooks.

For weeks Bath full-back Audley Lumsden made a play for a girl
who worked in our Members' Bar because he overheard Graham Dawe's cousin tell Graham and me that he knew her well
and that she had loose morals. In fact, what Graham's cousin,
a dentist, was telling us was that she had loose molars.

*   *   *

During a pre-match talk Jack Rowell referred to a certain scrum-half whose passing he thought was poor.

'Don't worry about what Warrilow does when he receives the ball and passes it,' Jack informed us. 'He couldn't pass wind.'

In the late seventies, when we had suffered many defeats at the hands of the slick, technically superior Welsh club sides, Roger Spurrell buoyed us up in the away-team dressing-room after a heavy defeat at Pandy Park in Cross Keys with stirring, poetic words to rival those Shakespeare penned for the Agincourt battle speech in *Henry V*.

'Think positive, lads. We're learning fast. Our day will come. Remember, the sun shines on every dog's arse at some stage in its life.'

In the mid-eighties we played the Royal Navy in an invitation cup tournament. The scores were level with five minutes to go when the floodlights failed, so we replayed the game the following day. Jack Rowell, not for the first time, put the situation into perfect perspective for us during his team talk.

'Think of an honest journeyman going fourteen rounds with Mike Tyson,' he said. 'He's given so much there is nothing left to give. What keeps him going is the knowledge that the final bell is less than five minutes away. Then, suddenly, the stadium lights fail. He has to go through it all again with Tyson the next day. Boys, they just won't fancy it!'

Sure enough, we won by forty points.

Nottingham, 1982. As we took to the field we could hear the Nottingham captain psyching up his team in the home dressing-room. The Nottingham lads echoed his words and shouted in unison each line in a higher key.

'I am the boss!'
'I am the unbeatable!'
'I am the maestro!'

Jim Waterman, Dave Trick and I sneaked up to their dressing-room door and, in the lull after the third chant, shouted at the tops of our voices: 'I am the walrus! Coo coo-ky choo!'

At no time was the inspirational influence of films more evident than during England's 11–0 victory over France at Twickenham in 1989. The night before the game we players sat in the TV lounge at our hotel and watched a video of the Arnold Schwarzenegger film *The Terminator*.

The next day, twenty minutes into the game, Mike Teague was dealt a vicious blow to the face in a line-out and his nose started to pour blood. The game carried on as the referee allowed England physio Kevin Murphy to run on to the pitch to attend to Mike.

'I ain't got time to bleed,' growled Mike, declining medical assistance and pushing Murph away.

Mickey Skinner was presented to the eldest son of the Prince and Princess of Wales, HRH Prince William, in the home dressing-room before an England international at Twickenham.

'Mr Skinner,' said Prince William, extending a hand in greeting.

'Afternoon, sir. How's it hanging?' replied Mick, shaking the hand of the young prince, whose equerry almost fainted on the spot.

After the game Prince William was brought into the England dressing-room to congratulate us on our victory over Wales and also to bid us farewell.

'Well done, Mr Skinner,' said the prince on being reintro-
duced. 'And before you ask, may I inform you it's hanging
very well.'

The equerry of the Princess of Wales came into our dressing-
room at Cardiff Arms Park following our 1989 defeat at the
hands of Wales, a result which saw us blow the Grand Slam.

'Her Royal Highness will be visiting the team in about
five minutes,' he said to captain Will Carling. 'She'll ask
you what your team have said about losing the game and
the Grand Slam.'

'When I tell her, do I have to leave out all the foul-mouthed
swearing?' asked Will.

'Of course,' said the equerry haughtily.

'In that case they haven't mentioned it.'

In 1986, following England's 29–10 defeat by France at the Parc
des Princes, the England team attended a dance in an up-market
hotel in the centre of Paris. The concierge came over to where
we were sitting and asked if some of us could help him as he
was having trouble with a couple of gatecrashers on the door.
'They are 'orri-bell. Gangsters, I theenk. They try to force
their way een.'

'What do they look like?' I asked as Peter Winterbottom,
Dean Richards, Gary Pearce, Gary Rees and I went with the
concierge to the reception door.

'Oooh, thees men are ugly. Zay 'ave very ugly and
frightening faces, like 'orri-bell monsters from space.'

We all braced ourselves, not knowing quite what to expect.

'These them?' I asked pointing to the two men banging on
the door.

'Yes. Ees them,' said the concierge, cowering behind as we
all fell about laughing at the sight of coach Roger Uttley and
Wasps' Paul Rendall banging on the glass door.

271

'Call the police,' I advised as we turned to rejoin the dance.

In 1995 I attended a sporting luncheon in Leeds. Following the speeches several of us sat signing the souvenir menus for table guests. A silver-haired man asked me to sign an extra autograph for his grandson, which I was pleased to do.

'Who are them two ah like seeing playin' for England?' asked the old boy.

'Will Carling and Jerry Guscott?' I ventured.

'Nay, lad. Two brothers, they are.' He looked up at the ceiling and bit his bottom lip as he thought.

As I was about to supply the names, he had a flash of inspiration. 'Rory Underwood and Tony . . . er, Tony . . . Bloody 'ell, what's 'is other name?' he asked, annoyed at his forgetfulness.

'Underwood?' I suggested.

'Aye, tha's reet. Underwood. Well done, lad. Ah'd a been trying to think of that lad's surname name all afternoon!'

We had seen a piece on the BBC's *Sportsnight* about Liverpool FC and the facilities in the dressing-rooms at Anfield. Each player had a hair-dryer next to his peg. This impressed Andy Robinson, who brought in a battered old hair-dryer and hung it from a picture hook above the plug point.

Roger Spurrell was the first to try it after a training session. It whirred into action, rattling and clanking like a Lancaster Bomber as it blew with hurricane force into Roger's blond locks. The rest of us retired to the bar for some light refreshment. When, after fifteen minutes, big Roger hadn't appeared, John Palmer and I went back to the dressing rooms, fearing he might have been electrocuted. As we opened the door we immediately knew the reason for Roger's non-appearance in the bar. The dryer had given him a new hairstyle. To his consternation he was now a dead ringer for boxing promoter Don King!

Jim Waterman jumped off the coach on our way back from a game in Bridgend to buy a copy of the *Glamorgan Gazette*. During the journey he read aloud a piece about a man called Ivor Jones, a former Bridgend lock of the 1930s who had worked as a circus stilt-walker for thirty-six years.

'He died last Monday. He's left his heart, lungs and kidneys to medicine and his old boots and shirt to the club's social committee,' read Jim.

'Who's he left his legs to?' shouted out Dave Trick. 'Swan Vesta?'

The great Australian David Campese is a player I respect and admire. Like Ian Botham or George Best, he's not afraid to speak his mind, even if he upsets one or two people in the process. To my mind Campese is one of the greatest rugby players there has ever been and, like Both and Bestie, he deserves his place in the hall of sporting greats not only for his brilliance at his chosen sport but for being a superb entertainer into the bargain.

In the 1987 World Cup in Australia and New Zealand Campese made a big impression on Bath coach Jack Rowell with his scintillating rugby. From the very first England game in Pool 1, which England lost 19–6 to Australia in front of a capacity crowd at the Concord Oval in Sydney, Jack wanted to bring David to England and sign him up for Bath for three years.

David Robson, who was assistant coach to Jack, learned that he was to sit next to Campese at an official dinner. Jack asked David if he would sound out Campese about the possibility of signing for Bath.

No sooner was the dinner over and David Robson back in his hotel room than his telephone rang.

'Did you get to speak to Campese about a possible move?' asked Jack.

'Yes,' said David. 'But he's had an offer to play in Italy for Milan and they're talking big money.'

'How much?' asked Jack, knowing that, while Bath never pay players, he might be able to fix Campese up with a job to equal the amount being offered. '£200,000,' said David ominously.

The line went quiet and David heard Jack gulp. 'Two hundred thousand?' he repeated, flabbergasted. 'Over three years that works out at just under £67,000 a year!' He whistled to himself. 'I haven't a clue where we could fix him up with a job paying that sort of a salary but I suppose it's not impossible,' he said, trying to be optimistic.

'Jack,' said David, interrupting the coach's train of thought.
'What?'

'The £200,000 Campese has been offered,' David ventured. 'It's not over three years. It's for five months!'

38

The Game of the Century

TALK TO any All Black and he will tell you he is sick and tired of hearing about the one game Brits always talk about. But that game was, to my mind, the greatest ever. It took place at Cardiff Arms Park on 27 January 1973, when the Barbarians beat one of the all-time great New Zealand sides by 23–11.

'You Brits always want to talk about that 1973 game because it's the only time you've really had the upper hand on an All Black side and run out comfortable winners,' the former New Zealand captain David Kirk once told me.

That's not strictly true. The British Lions and England have enjoyed victories over the All Blacks since then and I also recall Scotland being unlucky to draw 25–25 against New Zealand at Murrayfield in 1983. Though I take David's point that victories over the All Blacks by home sides have been few and far between over the years, the reason why we 'Brits', as David and his compatriots call us, are keen to talk about 'that game' is because it was such a classic match – a smooth-passing, side-stepping display of showmanship rugby in its purest form, which continually swept from one end of Cardiff Arms Park to the other.

Of course I was not involved in this greatest-ever game. I watched it as a boy and marvelled. In later years it was my good fortune to be able to talk to and even play against some of the men who took part in what is widely known as the 'game of the century'.

To say I marvelled is no exaggeration. No sooner was the game underway than Llanelli's Phil Bennett received the ball with twenty-nine men in front of him. Less than three-quarters of a minute later, following a fluid passing movement that made the ball look as if it were being pulled from one Barbarian to the next on elastic, Gareth Edwards bounced upright to his feet after scoring the most breathtaking try in rugby history.

'What a score!' Cliff Morgan, commentating for BBC TV, blurted out.

I wouldn't mind betting that to his dying day Cliff will regret coming out with something so staid, Victorian, wholly understated and lacking in descriptive prowess. Still, it's not easy to wax instantly lyrical when the breath has been taken from you by such an explosive and sensational start. That said, I have often wondered what that great giant of Welsh literature Dylan Thomas, who died twenty years before, would have made of it. In Cliff's defence, he had just rushed up to the commentary box to substitute for Bill McLaren, who had to stand down because of a worsening throat infection. Poor Cliff didn't even have an official team sheet or match programme to work from. The greatest-ever game in the history of rugby and he had to provide a commentary on what he saw unfolding live before him, backed by his own general knowledge of the players on the field. No notes.

It was Auckland's Bryan Williams who, in the opening encounters, whacked the ball deep into the Baa-Baas half. Phil Bennett caught the ball and began the move that led to that try.

In later years, when I met Phil, he told me he had noticed that the All Blacks always liked to converge quickly on the player in possession. Before the game he made up his mind that, if they did that to him, he would try to side-step them, which is exactly what happened. The All Blacks back row flew at Phil, he side-stepped every one of them and left them fingering Cardiff air.

Phil Bennett is so self-effacing that if he ever wrote an autobiography, he'd probably mention himself no more than twice. I told him I was amazed by his feints, side-steps and dummies. He blushed. 'It was down to the others,' he informed me modestly. 'In the 1973 game against the All Blacks we created space. The forwards were on the floor, their proper position. We told them, don't handle the ball. Win it and give it to us and we'll do the switching runs.'

As the move began, at breakneck speed, Phil passed to J.P.R. Williams. J.P.R. was of the same school of thought as Phil when it came to counter-attacking: side-step and then create space and go straight for the jugular.

Bryan Williams hit J.P.R. with one of his more gentle tackles, taking him out at the chin and neck, but not before J.P.R. had fired off a pass to Bristol hooker John Pullin.

John is a wonderful man and was a fine player but, on his own admission, he wouldn't know the difference between a side-step, a quickstep and a town-hall step. He remembers wishing that someone else more creative had received the ball at that moment. Instinct, however, told him he had to get rid of it quickly and, seeing John Dawes to his left, he passed immediately to the Baa-Baas and Wales skipper just as a flurry of black-jerseyed bodies brought him down. The flowing move and the scintillating pace carried on unabated.

John Dawes received the ball inside his own 22 and, in his own words, 'flew down that left flank as if my arse was on fire'.

In his TV commentary the ad-libbing Cliff Morgan credited John with 'a glorious dummy'. But, far from taking that accolade, John refutes it. The way he tells the story, he was looking for John Bevan, aiming to put the Cardiff man clear down the left flank. Suddenly he saw space in front of him. Phil Bennett had sucked in the All Black back row with his Lionel Blair footwork and there was no organised New Zealand defence to repel the counter-attack.

Dawes was on the point of feeding the ball to Bevan but thought better of it at the last moment, hence Cliff Morgan's inference that he had sold a dummy. Instead John saw the Llanelli flanker Tommy David appearing in support by his side and slipped the ball to him. By now the pace was even quicker.

Tommy almost bodged it by making an uncharacteristic poor pass to Derek Quinnell. In Tommy's defence Derek says he received the pass 'comfortably enough, at about eight inches below my knee and running at top speed. Whilst I was down there, I adjusted my bootlaces'.

Talk to any of those Barbarians today and they will tell you that Derek's 'over-the-heads lobbed pass' was intended for John Bevan. All except for Derek, that is. He is adamant that it was intended for the player who received it, Gareth Edwards. 'Gareth was screaming at the top of his voice for the ball as he saw space open up in front of him down our left flank,' Derek told me.

I have played enough rugby to know that the player in the best position to receive, screaming or not, is not necessarily the intended recipient of a pass. But Derek is bigger than me, so I'm not doubting his word.

Gareth Edwards could catch racing pigeons, he was that quick. On receiving the pass that was 'rightfully intended for him', he took off for the corner. He beat Grant Batty for sheer pace, no mean feat in itself, and, with a flying leap, touched down by the flag. In so doing he was hit with a last-ditch tackle and propelled through the air to his left. But immediately he hit the ground, he bounced to his feet, arms aloft and smiling. I'll never forget his expression.

From the point when Phil Bennett caught that ball to Gareth diving over the line to create the most fluid counter-attack in rugby history, the play took thirty seconds. It would take me longer to drive from one end of the Arms Park pitch to the other in my car!

As luck would have it, the move which led to the try that has been dubbed the most photogenic try in the history of rugby was so quick that it caught every press photographer on the hop. No one was in a position to immortalise Gareth going over. Fortunately BBC TV cameras were there to capture the historic moment for posterity. Cliff Morgan remembers the outside broadcast director that day, who hadn't seen the monitor because he'd been walking along the gantry to the commentary box, shouting to his cameraman, 'Did you get that? Tell me you got it!' and the camera operator bubbling with excitement and screaming back into his microphone, 'Yes! Yes! Yes!'

It's a good job he did. The BBC have sold getting on for 90,000 videos of the game and people still ask for it.

What that try exemplifies to me is a state of mind. That open space is open space, whether you're defending deep in your own half or attacking beyond the opposition's 20-metre line.

The try and the victory were all the more sweet because this particular game was a grudge match. These All Blacks were not like those we had known before and have met since, highly competitive but warm and wonderful off the field.

These were All Blacks who pushed aside and even verbally abused children who asked for their autographs. They were a top-class outfit but unbelievably arrogant with it and not beyond inflicting deliberate injury on an opponent in order to achieve victory. For pure flair I doubt whether we shall see a game to equal it. Each member of the Baa-Baas that day had different skills, yet they were complementary to one another and gelled magnificently as a team.

Cambridge University's Bob Wilkinson, one of the two uncapped players taking part that day, went on to play for Bedford and to win six caps for England. He tells me, however, that he suffered from the 'Orson Welles syndrome'. Like the great film director, Bob's crowning moment of glory came in a masterpiece just as his career was starting. Everything that followed, if not exactly an anti-climax, certainly never equalled it.

I met the All Black and former Counties stalwart Bruce Robertson during the British Lions tour of New Zealand in 1993. Bruce is now the coaching director of Auckland and played centre against the Baa-Baas that day. 'They talk about the game being quicker nowadays but that game was unbelievably fast,' recalled Bruce. 'When the move leading to that try swept down the pitch, I tried on numerous occasions to make a tackle but I was always one pace away from being able to do so.'

When I saw the game as a young boy, although I watched in amazement at the speed, skill and dexterity of both sets of players, soccer remained my big love. I didn't switch to rugby until leaving school three years later. In a way I'm glad. Such an historic and memorable match could easily have given me a false impression and clouded my judgment. If I had taken to rugby immediately after seeing the Barbarians against the All Blacks, I might have been quickly disappointed that rugby wasn't like this all the time and given up the game. It can happen so easily. As a

Buckingham Palace equerry once told me whilst accompanying a member of the royal family to a game at Twickenham, 'The Queen is under the impression that all of Great Britain smells of wet paint.'

For the benefit of Cliff Morgan and yourself, I went up into my loft at home to find the match programme of the great Barbarians v New Zealanders game of 1973. This is how they lined up.

Barbarians

15   J.P.R. Williams (London Welsh & Wales)
14   D.J. Duckham (Coventry & England)
13   S.J. Dawes (capt) (London Welsh & Wales)
12   C.M.H. Gibson (NIFC & Ireland)
11   J.C. Bevan (Cardiff & Wales)
10   P. Bennett (Llanelli & Wales)
 9   G.O. Edwards (Cardiff & Wales)
 1   R.J. McLoughlin (Blackrock Coll & Ireland)
 2   J.V. Pullin (Bristol & England)
 3   A.B. Carmichael (West of Scotland & Scotland)
 4   W.J. McBride (Ballymena & Ireland)
 5   R.M. Wilkinson (Cambridge University)
 6   T.P. David (Llanelli)
 8   D.L. Quinnell (Llanelli & Wales)
 7   J.F. Slattery (Blackrock College & Ireland)

New Zealanders

15   J.F. Karam (Wellington)
14   B.G. Williams (Auckland)
13   B.J. Robertson (Counties)
12   I.A. Hurst (Canterbury)
11   G.B. Batty (Wellington)

10   R.E. Burgess (Manawatu)

 9   S.M. Going (North Auckland)

 1   G.J. Whiting (King Country)

 2   R.A. Urlich (Auckland)

 3   K.K. Lambert (Manawatu)

 4   H.H. Macdonald (Canterbury)

 5   P.J. Whiting (Auckland)

 6   A.I. Scown (Taranaki)

 8   A.J. Wyllie (Canterbury)

 7   I.A. Kirkpatrick (capt) (Poverty Bay)

Replacement: GL Colling (Otago) for Going

Scorers

BARBARIANS 23: *Tries* – Edwards, Williams, Bevan, Slattery; *Conversions* – Bennett (2); *Penalty goal* – Bennett.

NEW ZEALAND 11: *Tries* – Batty (2); *Penalty goal* – Karam.

Referee

G Domercq (France)

It was traditional for the Baa-Baas to field one uncapped player against international touring sides. In this game it was to be Bob Wilkinson, the Cambridge University lock. In the end the game was unique at the time for the fact that the Baa-Baas fielded two uncapped players. Llanelli's Tommy David came in at blindside wing-forward as a late replacement for Mervyn Davies.

39

. . . And Finally

A TTENDING AS many games and sporting dinners as I do, I'm often asked who were the best players I ever competed against. On a number of occasions I've even been asked to compile my All-Time Greats XV. Up to now I have never done so, simply because such a task would require me to sit down and give considerable thought to choosing such a team. Due to the lifestyle I lead, I've never found the time.

When it came to writing this book, however, I decided to make the time. Now that my playing days are over, I felt it appropriate to end by selecting my All-Time Greats XV. It wasn't easy. I was fortunate enough in my career to play alongside and against most of the world's greatest rugby players of the past twenty years. I deliberated and pondered long and hard. For certain positions, I couldn't decide between two or three players and in the end went for the player that most suited the game plan I had in mind.

Here, then, is Coochie's All-Time Greats XV, selected from those I have had the honour of playing with or against.

Coochie's All-Time Greats XV

Full-back: **Serge Blanco** (Biarritz and France)

Ahead of his time. Superb vision, adventurous and full of the flair for which the French are renowned.

Right wing: **David Campese** (ACT, NSW, Milan and Australia)

Every sport needs one. Cricket had Botham, soccer had Best. Outrageous, naturally gifted, superbly entertaining. A rugby genius.

Right centre: **Philippe Sella** (Agen and France)

Simply the most consistent centre in the world. A great team player.

Left centre: **Jeremy Guscott** (Bath and England)

Grace, speed and skill. When there is deadlock, he'll produce something out of the ordinary to win the game. Also the most good-looking player I've ever seen.

Fly-half: **Michael Lynagh** (Queensland and Australia)

I deliberated for hours over this. It was Phil Bennett, then Barry John, then Gareth Davies. In the end Michael shaved it for being the best tactical kicker I've ever encountered. Not a fag-paper's width between the four of them, though.

Left wing: **Ieuan Evans** (Llanelli, Harlequins and Wales)
Has made more appearances than any other Welsh wing. The most tricky and elusive winger I have ever played with, he uses the ball to great effect. A marvellous tourist.

Scrum-half: **Gareth Edwards** (Cardiff and Wales)

Gareth was at the end of his career when I was starting mine. Even so, he had immense presence on the field and a never-say-die attitude. The all-round great rugby player. Quite brilliant.

Loose-head prop: **Fran Cotton** (Coventry, Sale and England)

Fran the man. A big, powerful man in a big position. No matter how tough and rough it became, he never flinched.

Hooker: **Phil Kearns** (NSW and Australia)

Phil exemplifies the typical Aussie hooker: strong, aggressive, positive when he has the ball in his hands. All action to the final whistle.

Tight-head prop: **Graham Price** (Pontypool and Wales)

The finest tight-head prop ever to put boots on, and a destructive scrummager whose power and skill destroyed numerous reputations and egos.

Lock: **Wade Dooley** (Preston Grasshoppers and England)

A big man whose strength was matched only by his bravery. Loyal to a fault, as any Hoppers fan will tell you.

Lock: **John Eales** (Queensland and Australia)

As a nineteen- to twenty-year-old John was far and away the best line-out jumper in the world. Injuries hindered his later career, but all who played against him agree that he was at the top of the ladder in terms of international class.

Flanker: **Peter Winterbottom** (Headingley, Harlequins and England)

I can never recall Peter playing badly for club or country. Not the most sociable of people, but a strong, gifted player I'd have with me any day.

Number 8: **Laurent Rodriguez** (Mont-de-Marsan, Montferrand, Dax and France)

Great player, great hands. Neat, skilful, fast and deceptively strong. He will produce something sensational and outrageous just when you need it to swing a game your way.

Flanker: **Michael Jones** (Auckland and New Zealand)

They broke the mould when they produced this wing forward. He elevated play in this position to a new level. Consistent and brilliant.

40

. . . And Absolutely Finally

**Five things I Would Change About the Game –
Right Now**

*(But let's see how long rugby's administrators take to get around
to it.)*

1. The wheeled-scrum law. Abolish it now. Recent legislation
demands that every time a scrum wheels, the referee must start
it again. This has resulted in scrums going on ad infinitum. Just
play on, for heaven's sake!

2. Remove the restrictions on players for off-the-field earnings.
Gordon Brown (Scotland and British Lions) accepted royalties
for a book to which he made a contribution in the late 1970s. He
was banned by the Scottish RU, even from coaching mini-rugby.
Years later that ban is still in force, despite attempts to have it
lifted. If I were 'Broon from Troon', I'd take the Scottish RU
to Strasbourg. Gordon is by no means unique. The message
to all unions is: move with the times and let players receive
the off-the-field earnings enjoyed by all other sportsmen and
women.

3. Let's see equality between the rugby-playing countries of the southern and northern hemispheres — in all matters.

4. Get rid of those grey, dour people who call for players to have a more 'professional attitude' and want to rid our game of its characters. True, the nature of rugby today demands that it be taken seriously but the disappearance of the colourful figures we have both on and off the field would vastly diminish the sport.

5. Find the person who invented the bleep fitness test for players. Take him to Bristol docks and have him hung, drawn and quartered.

I hope I've ended this book, not with a moan, but with some constructive ideas that would improve our game. Rugby may have its faults but to me it's the greatest game in the world and I hope that, by relating some of my favourite rugby stories, I have captured the 'crack'. To rugby players, officials (yes, you too) and supporters everywhere: enjoy your rugby, as I hope you have enjoyed my book.